Cars and People

✦

How to Put the Two Together

Anthony Douglas Ziegler

iUniverse, Inc.

New York Lincoln Shanghai

Cars and People
How to Put the Two Together

iUniverse, Inc.

For information address:
iUniverse, Inc.
2021 Pine Lake Road, Suite 100
Lincoln, NE 68512
www.iuniverse.com

Although this book is a work of nonfiction, the author employs the use of fiction to assist whenever necessary in illustrating specific views and ideas. The views expressed are for educational purposes only. Names, characters, places, and incidents either are products of the author's imagination or are used fictitiously. Any resemblance to actual events, locales, or persons, living or dead, is entirely coincidental.

ISBN: 0-595-32751-6 (pbk)
ISBN: 0-595-66681-7 (cloth)

Printed in the United States of America

Cars and People

Books by Anthony Douglas Ziegler

Cars and People; Pissing at 60 Miles an Hour
Drivetime; Finding a Way Home
Kamikaze Gods and Suicide Mules

Dedicated to my father, for teaching me how to eat an elephant.

Contents

Part V   *Knowing Your Prospects*

Preface

o o o o o o o o o o o o o o o o o o o o o o o o o o o o o o o o o o

"We are in the greatest business in the world. It's a business about cars and people. You just have to know how to put the two together."

—Mr. Empire

The pet rock was selling well and the buzz was out. Whoever thought of this ingenious way to pilfer the funds from every person trying to keep up with their neighbors? What sort of mind could bring the fire to this novelty item?

It was summer vacation and well before Christmas when my stepfather asked me to get rid of our rocks. They were leftover from the days when a construction crew had built our suburban neighborhood in Salinas, California. Dumped in a pile about four feet in circumference and a couple feet high, they were an eyesore in a backyard that knew nothing but such irritations.

"I don't care how you do it. Just do it," my stepfather demanded.

I was nine years old. Most of our neighbors knew me as the "quiet Tony." There was a "trouble maker Tony" who happened to live adjacently to us. He was about my age yet quite a bit taller and much louder. His mouth moved faster than his feet. He was always getting caught doing something wrong. I, on the other hand, was typically right beside him when the crime was being conspired and remained with him up to the moment that he began to call attention to the act. Once the hollering started you couldn't find me. I didn't run considerably faster, but I knew when to run.

My neighbor decided to help me dispose of the rocks by throwing them over my fence into other neighbors' yards. Their gardens, garage walls, and windows caught much of what was tossed. My stepfather suddenly cared about how I removed the rocks. "Find another way and do it alone."

We always had nearly empty spray paint cans stored on shelves in the garage. Usually the colors were not the most appealing. Typically, school bus yellow and variations of the same were in abundance because my stepfather drove a school bus for a living.

As much as I would like to say that I knew what I was doing when I began spraying the rocks yellow on one side only, I cannot. I did however spray them in that way, in amounts that were just enough to fill my wagon.

It wasn't uncommon for me to knock on neighbors' doors selling something. Cookies, candy, and raffle tickets were my typical wares. I became somewhat proficient in peddling whatever items various after-school functions I happened to be a part of had dreamt up.

From door to door I walked through our neighborhood alone, knocking and encouraging neighbors to buy my yellow rocks. It was to their benefit that I had "discovered gold in my backyard." It didn't matter what they paid. A dollar here. Two bucks there. I emptied my wagon and returned to fill it, only to empty it again the next day. This went on every weekday during the summer until there were no rocks left.

I knew people weren't buying the rocks because of their need for a half-painted rock. They bought them because I was cute in thinking that I was fooling them. They found it strange that this quiet kid could be so foolish to believe that they would fall for the idea that the rocks were actually gold. Another reason was that they were predisposed to buying rocks thanks to media conditioning regarding the pet rock. They had little trouble in doing so. I learned and understood this after the first full wagon was sold in short order.

Having no rocks left to sell and no money left to buy candy, I sat on my front lawn watching the girl across the street sell lemonade. Her father had built a pristine white lemonade stand for her. If you saw her stand, you could tell immediately that it was designed strictly for the sale of lemonade by a very young, adorable little girl. It was the type of scene that made a boy who showered once a week and wore hand-me-down clothes quite envious. To this day, whenever I start to feel jealous I still have visions of that girl, sitting behind her stand, selling everybody who passed by a cup of lemonade.

With the rocks gone a problem with snails in our backyard arose. I guess the snails had nowhere to live. They kind of came out of the rock pile area and took over every weed in the yard, board on the fence, and crack in the ground. If cute could work for rocks, it could work for snails.

With a couple boards nailed together, mother's favorite table cloth, some catsup, and a piece of painted cardboard reading, "B-B-Q Snails only $1.00," I attempted to destroy the neighbor girl's business. It wasn't long before I buried her. Sure, people still stopped for some lemonade. To my benefit, all of those who had stopped also came over to inquire about barbecued snails. I knew they wouldn't eat them. I soaked them in catsup, cooked them until they were chunks of blackened coal, and plopped them on a paper napkin with a fresh dollop of catsup on top. People bought them. They laughed their asses off and bought them. They took them home to show their friends and families what this "stupid little boy" was selling. I stayed home and counted their money.

The stories can go on. Rather than bore you with every one, I'll skip ahead to a time when I had run out of gas in Reno, Nevada. I was nineteen and on my own.

After working for a few different casinos, doing the only jobs that I could do, being under the wonderful age of twenty-one, I landed a job with the State of Nevada. I worked with acute and chronic care psychiatric patients on what was referred to as 8-South. Actually, they weren't considered patients. They were called clients. We worked for them. The majority of the clients had voluntarily placed themselves in our treatment. My title was "primary therapist." That's a nice title for a guy who encourages the clients to keep themselves clean by giving them access to showers, making sure they take their medications, teaching them how to complete daily tasks like tying their shoes and brushing their teeth, wiping whatever needed to be wiped when necessary, making sure they didn't screw the other non-responsive clients, and occasionally playing a little volleyball with them.

I spent five years interacting with people whose inability to adapt to the outside world kept them locked inside a micro social structure. In many cases they were afraid. They did not want to stay but the option of leaving and being by themselves was considerably more frightening. They would've rather been where they had some predictable routine in a place, where the majority of people who were around them were just as "normal" as they were.

Normal is a word whose definition changed for me while working with these folks. Perception became evident as a word that had a considerable impact on what normal truly meant. The majority decides what is normal.

Everything changes. The State of Nevada had some major budget concerns. Many people were laid-off or reassigned. It was always the people who hadn't been there very long. Forty percent of the "reassignments" were in the department of mental health. Made sense. Affect the people that we, as a majority, did not want to acknowledge existed, and they will go away.

Many of my coworkers were at the facility too long. Their tenure had jaded them to the point of becoming abusive. Not all. Many of them. There were some whom everyone knew to be verbally, physically, and oftentimes sexually abusive to some of the clients. The excuse was that they were burnt out from being lied to as well as physically attacked continuously. They were the care givers that the clients didn't trust. Their seniority protected their positions. Thankfully, a few very good people stayed as well.

I moved along with my life. I did not wish to leave. I had built relationships with many of the clients. Relationships where the foundation is mutual trust as well as the perception of trust are very strong.

Within a couple years of leaving I found myself on the phone with my father. I've always called him whenever I needed to make big decisions. He has helped me to reorganize my thoughts as well as my life on many an occasion. He's exceptional at these things. He's a car salesman.

"Why don't you sell cars?"

"Me? I'm not a car salesman."

It wasn't long after our phone conversation that I moved back to my hometown in California. I purchased a couple pairs of dress slacks, three shirts, a belt, three ties, and a nice pair of shoes with money I borrowed from him. I was hired at a dealership where two of the three Cs could very well have been convicts and cocaine. "If you can work for that store you can work anywhere" were words I'd heard time and again when I informed peers where I was working.

The time I spent on the "line" in that dealership helped shape me into the man I am today. It was more of a pounding than a subtle shaping. I am grateful for what I gained by working there. It's always good to learn what not to do when you need to understand what should be done. In the words of Arlo Guthrie, "You cannot have a light without a dark to stick it in."

I moved up quickly. I became the top dog and the target of the slower salesmen. My family grew and our financial position improved by incredible measures. My car sales career began as something that any sales-oriented professional would be jealous of. Funny, because I did not realize how extraordinary my climb to the top was, until I was off the mountain, looking back at the peak.

Ten years passes quickly when you love what you do. Nine years went just like that. One was hard. It was the year that I learned the most. The year that I decided I would no longer laugh at jokes that weren't funny simply because the person who told the joke signed my check. I will no longer laugh when people hurt other people to feel better about their own failures. The next ten years will pass quicker than the last.

I've taken this last year to spend with my family, touring the states while looking for a better place to raise my children. The journey has allowed for many opportunities to take time out and reflect upon the career which I enjoy so much. I've returned to reading the journal which I have kept since my first day in the business. This review of the events as well as the people I have known became the spark that fueled my desire to share with others what I have experienced.

The following pages are the first in a series which I intend to publish and spread. This is what I intend to give back to the business to show my gratitude for what it has done for me. Thank you for buying this book and taking the time out to improve yourself. Whether you are an old pro, a green pea, or a customer looking for insight into the strange and enchanting world of car sales, you will be entertained.

For those of you who are thinking of entering into a new career of car sales, I applaud you. You're the light that is coming in to brighten the business. Your input may change it ever so slightly into a more respected, positive business.

For those of you who have been in the business for under a year I encourage you to never give up. There is something fresh and new around every corner. You can advance to whichever position you wish with continued training, a great attitude, and a management team that values your skills. By purchasing this book you have shown your commitment to honing these skills. You will make a difference.

Then there are my guys. Those of us who have been in the business through one or more selling cycles. We've seen the ups and downs. We've watched new green peas come and fade. We've experienced managers being blown out on Mondays. The training trends. The gung-ho closers. I commend you. You are the difference. Dealers have made money on your backs. You have paid for their swimming pools, yachts, and summer vacations. You have put their kids through college. You help make this industry the absolute best industry to be a part of.

It takes us all. We are the tools of the trade. We cannot do every job with only one tool. We need each other to turn to, train with, and bounce objections off of. We are the team that cannot be beat. Together we will all make a difference in our own and the customers' lives.

Why write this book and make it available for the mass market to read? Simply put, to help improve our business. When you have finished reading and began applying what we have discussed within these pages, you will be a more confident as well as competent salesperson. Let's face it: There are no books that are specific to selling cars which share more than the basics. Nothing in the bookstore delves into the behavioral side of what's going on between the buyer and seller while the steps are taking place. Nothing until now.

When I began in the business I looked for anything that would help me. I found plenty of books aimed at selling everything but cars. The majority made claims of great wealth and secret systems which had no relationship to my world.

Not only are they thick with irrelevant information, but their wordiness alone breeds failure when we do not finish a particular book.

I turned to books marketed toward customers regarding "how to buy a car." All of which seemed to be written by pissed off car salesmen who couldn't sell enough cars to keep their jobs or by people who were given the "mushroom treatment" (kept in the dark and fed shit) the entire time they were in the car business. The information given is typically inaccurate and completely short-sighted. It is within the pages of those books that the smoke and mirrors, what the majority believes happens behind that mysterious door of management, is created and exaggerated. Nobody wins when nobody knows what is truly going on.

I intend to lift that smoke of secrecy and allow everyone in to understand not only "how" people sell cars but "why" we do. Not just the money side of why but the behavioral side. The side that can withstand the negative reinforcement in this social world we live in. The side with skin so thick, when it's asked "What do you do for a living?" it can say "I sell cars" and not have to take the myriad of questions or insults that typically follow.

My wife would say that she has often wished I would not tell people what I do for a living. She would prefer if I didn't feel as if I have to defend my career choice. As well, she wouldn't want me to feel badly by putting my tail between my legs and allowing other people's ignorance about the business to stand out unchallenged.

If you have purchased this book as a means of getting a better deal when you buy a car, then you will. I only hope that you use this information in good conscience. The truth alone will not help you as much as your application of conscience could.

If this book is to be your training material as a car salesperson then I am in deep gratitude for your belief in what I have to share with you. The learning experiences that I have had are yours to enjoy, learn from, and share as your own.

In every case, it is learning what we don't know that keeps our mind growing and our thoughts fresh. Together we will take a look at stereotypes and rebuild an industry that is long overdue for a straight approach. This can only be achieved with your willingness. Everyone must buy in.

Introduction

We're going into the city. It's about thirty miles away and the traffic could be hell. It usually is. There are eight of us and we're all going to leave at the same time but we each have our own transportation. There will be traffic concerns: accidents, road blocks, construction, detours. We have plans to meet at a specific place and time, which we'll do our best to do. Unfortunately, something always comes up.

If we take the same vehicle we may meet our objective. We would arrive together. Road hazzards could receive proper attention, offering eight different viewpoints regarding how to best overcome and avoid them altogether, now as well as in the future.

We could learn alternative routes from those who may have traveled these streets before. We all know different areas and our strengths come from not only what we have learned but who our teacher was. It shows in our listening to others and how we apply what they have to share. It is in our intuitive abilities, understanding when to use our new routes and when not to.

Within these pages are personal experiences that I will share with you. These are not my words alone. From my father to my first closer in the business, I have taken words and events that others have shared. The seven team members who I had the pleasure of beginning my career with on the line each had their influence, with their stories and phrases for conquering specific situations, which I have picked over in necessary times. I have listened to dealer principals and general sales managers share their past glories, as well as failures, and have used what they have added to help myself and my peers.

These words are practices and principals which have evolved over years into the car sales process. They exist because they work. Through repeated usage they may have changed a bit, their edges rubbed smooth, their appearance not as flawed. But they are essentially the same.

Nobody owns the steps to the sale, various ways to overcome objections, or the redirecting closes. They are a compilation of ghosts that have ridden in the same car, offering alternatives to the quickest way into the city. They are words we all share. If they can close a deal, then they become "mine." I offer you those that I have made mine via repeated use.

I will discuss who the car salesperson and the customer are. We will review habits, both good and bad. We will take a quick look into various mediums of advertisement and what they mean to us. I will help you through the interviewing process so you can land your position with the right store. Finally, we will dive into the deal and explore the behavioral elements as well as learn the steps to the sale and why they are essential.

I have never been short on personal beliefs, or reluctant to share them with all who sit still long enough for me to do so. Unlike other writers who may profess to be "unbiased" or journalists who hide their beliefs skillfully within the context of the words, I intend to share my views openly. I refuse to pull any punches.

Some of my language may be a bit strong. I have always been a very passionate person. Everyone has passion for something. I have a passion for what I do and what I believe could be accomplished with a reasonable amount of careless abandon.

Read these pages front to back the first time through. Allow me the opportunity to build you up with the seeds planted in each section. When you finish, keep this book in your office so you may go back as often as you see fit to harvest whichever ideas you need. Write notes within the margins and highlight passages you feel will help you on your way to improving the way we do business.

Encourage your coworkers to purchase their own copies. By talking over the ideas within these pages among your coworkers and peer groups, you will be able to take that journey into the city and arrive in the manner a team should: Together.

I hope that people other than car salesmen buy and read this book. We owe it to ourselves, as professionals, to tell it our way. This is *our* "how to sell a car" book.

PART I

The Salesperson, The Customer, & Stereotypes

○ ○

"Your friends are the dullest dogs I know. They are not beautiful: they are only decorated. They are not clean: they are only shaved and starched. They are not dignified: they are only fashionably dressed. They are not educated: they are only college passmen. They are not religious: they are only pewrenters. They are not moral: they are only conventional. They are not virtuous: they are only cowardly. They are not even vicious: they are only 'frail.' They are not artistic: they are only lascivious. They are not prosperous: they are only rich. They are not loyal: they are only servile; not dutiful, only sheepish; not public spirited, only patriotic; not courageous, only quarrelsome; not determined, only obstinate; not masterful, only domineering; not self-controlled, only obtuse; not self-respecting, only vain; not kind, only sentimental; not social, only gregarious; not considerate, only polite; not intelligent, only opinionated; not progressive, only factious; not imaginative, only superstitious; not just, only vindictive; not generous, only propitiatory; not disciplined, only cowed; and not truthful at all: liars every one of them, to the very backbone of their souls."

—George Bernard Shaw
Man and Superman

Who's Who

There are two of us, and we think we know who we are. Either we're the car sales-man whose role it is to steal every dime from anybody who walks by or we're the customer who is constantly covering our wallet.

In this section we will discuss our role in the deal. Whether we are buying or selling has little to do with a behavior we share. Let's face it. We are both giving false information during the entire transaction in some manner or another. Maybe we are not intending to do so. It could be the fact that we simply do not know the correct answer to the question being asked that makes us give an answer we feel best suits our situation at the time.

Whatever the reason we must realize that we are designed to defend ourselves. It is within our making that we justify and rationalize to keep ourselves from feel-ing negatively.

A good friend of mine once stated that when asked whether we had a good day or a bad day we would complete a series of subconscious gyrations and answer accordingly. A good day would be a day where we had imposed our will on another and had come out victorious more often than not. Is this who we are?

Take note during a normal day of work or play. Ask yourself, in every interac-tion you have, who was trying to impose their will upon the other. Try to keep a conscious tally of sorts every time you win or lose. How does it make you feel after each situation? When your day is over, ask yourself, was it a good or bad day that you had, and why?

How could it be any different if we were to intentionally place ourselves within a situation where our "livelihood" were at risk? The level of stress can only be exaggerated when money is involved. Think about this: the number one rea-son for divorce is money concerns. How many liars are there in a divorce court?

Who is the car salesperson? Do we know how their livelihood is effected by us buying the vehicle or not? We could jump to answers filled with rationalizations and justifications quickly here. However, perhaps we should look a little closer.

I'm going to tell you a story of a man that I met. We'll call him Willy. He had been working with my father as a salesperson for about a year when I first met him. Standing 6' 7", his somewhat dopey appearance was only exaggerated by his slow gate. He was one of those people who constantly tucked his shirt tail in while he limped along, favoring one leg one day and the other leg the next.

Willy had a spectacular smile, if you could get him to show it. About 55 years old and divorced three or so times, he felt that he had little to smile about and constantly shared that opinion. He would sit around between deals and discuss the women that had taken his money. It was always about how he became a multimillionaire time and again. Each divorce cost him his fortune. To get him to smile I'd play along, encouraging him to get him worked up so he would let me have the customer that walked on the lot during his story. It worked often.

It seemed that he had invented quite a few items in his life that were contracted through a government agency or two. Strange items that sounded far too sci-fi to exist. Conspiracy was always a topic. I felt Willy had lost it. He was nuts. Plain and simple. Delusions of grandeur. Flight of ideas. You name it.

One day we had to deliver a car to a customer's house together. I was following to bring him back to the store. It was hot that day so after picking him up we decided to get a quick beer. One turned into two and so on. Pretty soon Willy was talking about this ice cream scoop with Teflon and a warming device that he had patented. "Actually, it was only the little red button" he patented, he had clarified while going on about how he had thousands of them in storage. I tried to keep a straight face but couldn't. I found myself laughing and drawing all his stories out to be torn apart.

It looked like he was going to cry when he turned away from me and emptied his bottle. "Come on," he said, walking toward the parking lot without looking me in the eye.

He drove. We stopped along the way at a storage facility on the edge of town. Imagine my surprise when he opened not one, but two separate storage warehouses with cases stacked floor to ceiling. He pulled a case down. Opened it. Handed me a Teflon ice cream scoop and said, "Keep the whole damn case."

It wasn't more than a week later that Willy brought in a sort of "yearbook" from a government agency. One of the sections had a four-page report complete with photographs of a younger Willy shaking hands with very impressive looking people. The captions stood out strongly. The article completely backed every delusional reference he had ever shared.

Why do I mention this? Perceptions. We jump to what we feel is possible and the rest we call lies. If we don't see ourselves capable of something, we shackle others within our shortcomings. It isn't enough that we don't believe in our own ability to achieve under certain situations, we must keep others from doing better than we have allowed for ourselves.

I'm not saying that Willy only tells the truth. I've grown to know him over the past 10 years. He'll be the first to admit he's a liar. But only when it suits him.

Willy is just one of many car salespeople. He's an example of what type of person *could be* a car salesperson. There are many others. Your neighbor. Your father. The kid who used to cut your lawn. The retired civil servant. The factory worker. The self-employed contractor. The elementary schoolteacher. The lawyer. The french fry technician. The maid. The plumber. The musician. The tailor. The fishing boat captain. The waiter. The produce manager. The dentist. Just a few more examples of some of the many people I've known who decided to sell cars.

What does your average car salesperson make? Better yet, how much money do you think a salesperson should be paid per deal? What do you think the profit on a $35,000 vehicle is? Take a pen and write your answers on the inner flap of this book. It will be nice to look back at them from time to time. If there are numbers there already because this book is borrowed, please use the back flap until you purchase your own copy. By the time you finish reading this book you may adjust your figures.

If I told you that the average in my store was about $35,000 a year, what would you think? Sounds okay, doesn't it? How about the top producer in a store has been known to make upwards of $120,000 a year? Sound better? Keep a few things in mind. Over 75 percent of all car salespeople who are green to the business quit within the first year. An average store turns 70 percent of its sales force over every year. The average car salesperson is scheduled to work 61 hours a week but works an additional 9 hours. The average car salesperson spends over 65 hours a year with formal sales training and product knowledge. The average car salesperson sells 11 cars a month. The average "mini-deal" (amount paid for a commission under payable gross) is less than $100. How many cars would you need to sell at $100 per vehicle to survive?

So who is the customer? There is an expression in the business that I do not enjoy hearing. Like many cliches and quotable quotes, it wouldn't exist if it weren't true in some part. "Buyers are liars." Let's face it, people are liars because of the conditions we impose upon them. Given these conditions, we should know not to ask the wrong questions or we will get answers we do not want to hear. We put them on the defensive and we must face the consequences of such a poor move on our part.

The customer is as predictable as we are. Their weakness is easily understood. They operate out of fear. Not exclusively, yet the majority of their decision-making ability is sparked from it. They will buy or not buy because of it. They will buy when they are afraid they will never see this deal again. They will not buy when they fear they are paying too much.

Americans know fear. We have been force fed fear since our births. The media shovels fear down our throats (amid occasional breaks regarding what we should consume). If we wear the right clothes we'll get laid. If we walk down the wrong streets we'll be killed. If we don't buy a big-screen television we'll miss out on the interest-free grace period and have to go to friends' houses for the playoffs. We'll get drunk because we're so damn boring and die driving home alone in our shitty cars.

Our parents began by introducing us to fear. Maybe it's their fault that we make the wrong choices. "Don't talk to strangers" and "if you hold that expression long enough your face will stay like that."

Most of us can remember hearing stories of razor blades in Halloween candy as children. My parents would not let me eat the candy until it was thoroughly inspected. The unwrapped candies were tossed in the trash. Every year the story was told of some child who did not listen to his parents and swallowed a razor blade. He bled to death in minutes.

Strange how this rumor begins. In the last four years the only recorded incident of tampered Halloween candy came from a situation where the child was poisoned by a family member. That true story didn't get nearly as much exposure as the fairy tale version. The media has allowed us to understand fear by using it to control what we watch and when we come home, afraid we'll miss something on television if we do not adhere to a strict time schedule.

Millions of teenage girls are afraid that they are not acceptable if they do not look like the waifs found on nearly every page of any magazine targeted toward a teen readership. The models are often found touting some miracle diet with their eighty-six pound chassis. Later in life they can often be seen in adult magazines reflecting on their bulimic or anorexic days. Meanwhile teenage suicide appears to be disproportionately on the rise if you ask the news channels. Or is it?

Do you have daughters? What is your fear? What would you do to keep your family safe?

Fear is what the customer is used to making decisions out of. Maybe it is a comfortable excuse for the future if we make the wrong decision today. We can easily remind ourselves and others that we made the decision hastily, out of no fault of our own, due to our intense fears triggered by uncontrollable factors.

With this said I give you the story of Joe Customer. Joe is a regular visitor to every salesperson. He says, "If you make me a deal I will buy from you right now." Sounds like Joe is being fair. He believes that he is every car salesperson's perfect situation; a quick, painless deal.

The problem is that he has placed burdens on the business. The car salesperson takes the "offer" to his manager, who must decide if Joe is telling the truth. Herein lies the problem. If Joe is presented a deal he will undoubtedly ask for another few bucks off. This means that not only did Joe lie because he is not buying yet, but that he believes the salesperson is not being completely honest with him, as there must be a few dollars left to grab.

Had the salesperson left some "extra" room in the deal to give to Joe when he asked for it, wouldn't the salesperson be lying in returning the deal to Joe as a "fair" deal? What if the salesperson put "extra" money in the deal just in case, and Joe agreed to its structure? How would that make the salesperson feel about himself?

It has been my experience that when this happens, and it happens often enough, the customer proves he lied by walking out the door without holding up his end of the bargain.

It is obvious to see where the customer forced the sales person to lie. Do we do this sort of thing in our everyday lives? Isn't it easier to deal with what we know, even if we don't like it, than with the unknown? When you have attended a meeting, your first day of school, or a business luncheon, who do you sit with? I would wager that you allow yourself the company of someone you know. We even choose to sit with people we don't like over people we don't know. What are we afraid of? How do we stop this cycle? Which part of the cycle are we responsible for?

Why Stereotypes Exist

Guess what folks? Stereotypes exist because they're true. At least they were at one point in time. They were true enough to create a large enough scale pattern for enough people to share the stereotype with one another and find it appropriate. It worked. It was true. It made sense.

Maybe times have changed. The stereotype is now a slanderous or politically incorrect entity. It reminds us of what could have been true regarding our ancestors or relatives. Do you think that remark has made a blemish somewhere in the foundation of following generations? You bet it has. It's there. It's eating away at us quietly, and all we need someone to do is mention it and we are screaming. A nerve has been struck.

Have you ever been in a situation where you are asked a very personal question regarding another person? The person asking the question, say your girlfriend or spouse, asks you to be truthful and answer this personal question. You do so and that person's head spins. The truth wasn't what they wanted to hear was it? You thought it was until you mentioned it. They became defensive regarding it didn't they? You are so right on that it hurts and they deny it.

"How does my ass look in these jeans?"

"Do you think I'm fat?"

"Is she prettier than me?"

That's what stereotypes do. They remind us of our flaws or our fears and we become so busy denying their truth that we cannot do anything else. We can no longer think logically and we must defend ourselves with unbridled ferocity.

I go to parties with my wife and hear about how car salesmen are liars and thieves. I become enraged. I defend the business I love by any means necessary. Occasionally I find one person to buy into what I am saying about how the business has changed so drastically by the difference I make. I bring that person into the dealership and I shred them. I am the stereotypical car salesman.

What stereotype do you fear the most? Which one is not true any longer?

Stories

Stories sell cars.

We can pretend that the steps to the sale alone can give us the knowledge we need to outsell our peers. Maybe lots of hard work grants us an extra sale here and there. Some smart work adds another sale. We get the sales that everyone expects us to get. The sum of this is just above average and we become the guy to beat in the store.

What about the world? How can we separate ourselves from the pack to such a degree that everyone will take notice? Is it in our actions or our final sale numbers? I feel it is within our stories.

I call these stories "life song." It is the music we hear playing faintly in the back of our heads when we recall our past experiences. The songs that played while we grew up driving fourteen hours in the back of a pick-up truck, rolling down the highway when it was still legal to do that sort of thing. Remember the moldy smell in the "way back" of mom's station wagon while we traveled across America during that special summer vacation? These are the stories that separate you from the pack. They give you an extra dimension. You become almost human with these stories as the customer begins connecting with a familiar side of you. You and he are so much alike that he may be persuaded at times by encouragement that you give.

This is where I want to be as soon as I can without looking or sounding too eerie. We must share some relevant behaviors as well as similar past experiences. Within these stories we will outsell the next guy and increase our gross profit. Try to recall your "life song" and share it with your customers whenever you see fit.

During this book I will share my stories. These are stories that either I have lived or I have borrowed but told enough times that they have become my own. I may have told these stories so often that I have forgotten whether they are my actual experiences or not. They may be someone else's stories, but they work well enough that I keep them in my repertoire. Use whichever stories you wish. I give them to you. They are yours now.

Before You Step On the Lot

○ ○

"It was easy. I just chipped and brushed away everything that wasn't an angel."

—Diane Arbus
(when asked how she sculpted such a beautiful angel)

The Foundation to You

I'd like to begin in a very analytical way, by discussing a variety of concerns that you may wish to consider prior to stepping on the lot for the first time. In a moment we'll go through each one of them and I'll pose questions for you to ask yourself. Although there is always something to learn when reviewing these topics, I would discourage making your decisions based entirely on what you read or the concession you come to by pondering these topics.

Where do you want to sell? What type of customer demographics would your personality be best to sell to? Would you do better in an economy brand dealership or a high line? What kind of image does the dealership have, and will it be improved by your working for them? Have you heard good things about a dealer in your area that has a very strong community presence? These questions need to be answered.

Before we begin, are you already employed at a dealership? Are you a "green pea"(new to the business)? If so, you need to believe that you have within you a wonderful mind that has already navigated this questioning process, subconsciously making the right decisions for you. You wouldn't have visited and applied to a dealership that you'd heard bad stories of unless your ethics are equal or the stories acceptable, be they true or false. I'll say it time and again: believe in your hunches. We make great subconscious choices.

I believe that a lot of this has proven evident via the incredible turnover in our business. Many people quit the car business after their second dealership. They just do not "have what it takes." Maybe they sold a few at the first dealer and something clicked. They thought they could sell anything, and probably could, but left the first dealership for a different demographic to sell toward, ended up clashing with a manager or owner, their positive attitude faded, they knew too much, or for just about any other reason, they performed poorly. They quit. They give up instead of trying another store. It's over for them.

I have three words to say to anyone who decides they are ready to quit. Try. Try. Try. Try once. Try twice. Try again. Every time you make a change, remember to do so for the right reasons. Only change after you determine that you cannot accept what is happening where you are. It takes three weeks to catch up. You have to build your momentum and learn your new store. Three weeks' income momentum is a lot to give up over an ego battle or some petty concern that you can easily overlook. But if you must leave, try another store with a different type of vehicle and customer demographic. If that doesn't work then you may change again.

Intuition

I cannot stress enough what intuition can do for you. Believe in it. If you are presently working at a dealership and in reviewing these questions you decide that you must make a change, please reconsider and try to achieve where you are at after completely reading this book and working the basics to their fullest. Believe in your intuition. You are working at that store for a reason. Something brought you there. Ride it out and give it your best shot. If you feel you must move on after doing so then so be it. But do not quit tomorrow.

For those of you who are green to the business and have not been hired yet, feel free to put extra weight in what conclusions you come to in this section. Allow your feelings to guide you. Have faith that you will make the right choice. When you do, work smart and do not give up no matter the obstacle. Give yourself the time it takes to succeed.

Attitude

I interview people regularly for their new occupation. They come to me and say things like, "Well, my wife left me. My dog died. My neighbor hates me. I lost my last job for stealing. My children ran away with their teacher. My mother won't return my calls. I might as well be a car salesman." Believe it or not, that's true. Maybe a bit exaggerated, but true nonetheless.

If this is you please find another occupation.

A positive attitude is the first attribute to have. It's not something that can be purchased. It cannot be faked for any prolonged period of time. Sure you can walk around with a smile and try to talk the talk. After a few days of no income and wondering why everyone is saying "No" to you, before you ask them a question you will find yourself stalking the sales manager on the desk. Eventually you'll explode and throw your keys at him. It is best to approach your new role with a cheerful attitude.

They say a positive attitude is contagious. I believe this to be true. I also believe that a positive attitude is very much appreciated. Especially in a role where we hear "No" far more than we'd prefer to.

If you are a seasoned professional you are familiar with how attitude effects your ability. You have found yourself running scared after selling fifteen cars the first week of the month and nothing since then. The last day of the month comes along and you are one unit away from your bonus. You push harder out of desperation. It is apparent. Your face reflects the obvious and your attitude is anything but positive. If you make a deal it's because the customer has a need with time restraints or feels he can take advantage of you on the last day of the month. It surely is not due to your ability to think straight or your wonderful attitude.

Whenever I need an attitude adjustment I buy a new suit. I enjoy looking good. The feel of new clothes reminds me that I am fortunate to be in such a great business that affords me the luxury of changing my wardrobe on a whim.

Ups and Downs

One way to ensure a good attitude is to have plenty of money in savings to get you through the initial training period. Whereas this would be ideal, it isn't always practical. Most of us don't decide to become a car salesman when we're knocking down all the money and have very few obligations. It's the other way around; no money and all the responsibility you can find.

Prepare for the ups and downs. When you've made the money and you have your bills paid, put some aside for the downtime. It will come. The business is cyclical. You'll have a bad month or two if you stay in the business for any period of time. You may be the exception and it may never happen, yet if it does you need to be prepared.

Career vs. Job

Good news! You've invested money. This is the first step toward a career. Whether you go to University of Yada Yada or School of Hard Knocks, education is important. Since there really isn't a vast amount of available resources one would typically find for many other careers, you have taken one of the only steps you can; you bought this book. Thank you, by the way, for doing so.

Having a career means you want to work. It means you wake up in the morning and head out for the day not focused so intently on time. You go to the office and you love what you do so much that the day slips past you. You have fun. Maybe you meet someone new, make a friend, or make a difference in somebody's life.

What's a job? Something you have to do. Something you resent. A way to pay bills. People with jobs clock in and out. They show up on the hour and leave the same way.

Floor Systems

There are two primary floor systems operating within most dealerships today. Both systems have their advantages and disadvantages. I will discuss each one so that you understand them both when you make your decision as to where you wish to work. I will say that I have worked both of these systems as well as a hybrid system. I like the hybrid system as it incorporates elements of the two primary systems.

Let's discuss the "straight sell" system first. Sounds just like it is: A straight sell plan is where a single salesperson takes the customer through the entire deal, front to back. You have the ability to complete the transaction in its entirety. From the initial hello to the handshake close, you are responsible. Most of the time the customer does not meet anybody else prior to entering the F&I office to complete his paperwork.

A positive facet is the control issue. Once you have control of the customer you can maintain it throughout the sale. If the customer has given you information which will work in the close but you have no idea of its importance until the opportunity presents itself, you will have the ability to recall it and use it when appropriate. If you had turned this customer to someone else, then your opportunity as well as your control can and often will vanish. Having the reigns the entire time builds confidence and credibility in you. The customer witnesses the fact that the dealership holds you as a respectable individual of some high esteem. Why else would they allow you to negotiate the deal for them?

A disadvantage in this type of system is the lack of teamwork. Maybe we feel that nobody else can do what we can. We let a customer leave, believing that he will return instead of turning this customer as we should. We do not offer anybody else a shot at the customer because a turn often means that we must split the deal. Why split it if the customer is going to be back?

Unfortunately, this happens often in many straight sell stores. The customer is not spun prior to leaving and doesn't return. We are letting our income walk away out of pure arrogance. We must get over this. We cannot determine who will buy or when they will buy. We do not know this.

I've had my name associated with some part of over 22,000 vehicle sales. I can't tell you who's gonna buy and who's gonna be back. I'm always amazed when somebody that I have let leave returns to see me. It makes me wonder what the planets are doing. I don't let people leave easily. When they go they're usually gone.

This is where the other floor system works well. In a "T. O." (or "turn over") system, every customer is worked by their salesperson right up to and including the tour of the dealership. They are brought inside and usually spun by the first pencil to a "manager." Usually manager is a title only, as he works mainly as a closer. He may have a desk manager who calls the shots, or he calls them himself. His primary function is to train his staff on how to turn their customers in a manner that complements his abilities.

Everybody is turned in this system. They are turned and it does not mean that a salesperson loses half his deal. They get it all. This is also a negative since the salespeople become lazy and reliant on the closers' abilities. They begin to short-cut their responsibilities in the deal, trying to rush more customers to their manager.

While it is wonderful to have every customer turned prior to leaving, rewarding a salesperson when he did not fulfill his role adequately only breeds ignorance. It allows salespeople to rely on others for their income. When people begin taking short-cuts they begin pointing fingers when the deals do not close. They do not want to accept the blame. It couldn't be them. It must have been something the closer did or did not do.

Remember this: a close is a natural end to a good presentation. A close with high gross is a natural end to a great presentation. Start short-cutting your presentation and you will short-cut your paycheck. Do not leave any zeros off the end of your money!

I like to work a system that encourages the salespeople to use their minds. I hold them accountable for the entire sale, as in a straight sell system. If they do not finish the deal they must turn to another salesperson. They are now married. If the new salesperson cannot progress the deal I will turn the customer to a third person on exit, usually a floor manager who roves around the dealership looking for scraps. He is paid on the number of deals he closes with bonuses based on average front end gross. His ego lives off the close.

I spiff my guys for spinning customers. Half a deal is better than no deal. Besides, think of it this way: There are ten salespeople and each salesperson gets ten customers during a normal weekend. If nobody spins then we only had ten opportunities. If everybody spins evenly, we would each get twenty. We would work twice as many customers. We'd be fresher. Well warmed up. It's a numbers game. The more people you are able to work, the more deals you will undoubtably make.

Highline vs. Budget

Some people say that high line car buyers are a different breed. They have the money and they didn't get it by throwing it around. They're careful when they spend it and they expect service. They'll pay for good service. Give them the experience that they think they deserve and you have a chance at getting their money. Since they're usually fairly smart, try and pull the wool over their eyes and you'll be standing outside on your day off waiting for them to show up to buy a car at pennies over invoice. If you're lucky they'll call you and let you know they bought somewhere else, from someone else. If you're not you'll turn blue holding your breath for them to return, then you'll see them drive by in a car they purchased elsewhere.

Budget car buyers are often credit challenged or cash poor. They may be first-timers or strictly payment sensitive. Either way this does not mean that they are not educated enough to know when you're lying. They may not ask many questions and they may not be able to calculate a payment within reason, but they do know that a stereo upgrade shouldn't cost them $2,000.

As with either case you should decide what you will work best with. Keep in mind that stereotypes are a good foundation for what you have to work with. People may do what we expect them to do.

Sell What You Know

What kind of car do you drive? Do you like it? What vehicles did you grow up around? What did/do your family members drive? What would you feel comfortable representing?

Stories sell cars. The family vacations that you and your family have taken could give other families insight as well as build common ground between you and the customer. Common ground is important in helping the customer feel calmer and allowing him to offer further information which you may be able to use to land him on the right vehicle and close the deal. You have to be able to relate your life stories when appropriate.

Some people should not sell certain vehicles. I do not understand how a Pearl Harbor survivor would want to sell Japanese-made vehicles, for instance. If you happen to be such a person, doing such a thing, then perhaps you are the exception. Maybe you are an exceptional salesperson to begin with and you would be selling even more vehicles if you focused on selling a vehicle you could feel better with yourself around.

I believe you should drive what you sell. Don't go out and buy a new car just yet. Be aware that your customers may see you driving somewhere. What type of image would you like them to see? How much more could you share about your personal experiences with a specific vehicle that you drive in your daily life, compared to one that you're only familiar with for brief moments on any given day?

At my local bank there is a man who handles the "personal finance department." He helps people invest their money. Though his clothes seem appropriate, his appearance and vehicle do not. He wears a shirt and tie. He's got to be at least three-hundred pounds overweight and maybe five feet, seven inches tall. He is constantly stuffing his face with fast food from the nearby mall food court and tucking his shirt in as he walks. The vehicle he drives is a 1978 Honda with dents, rust, and chipped paint.

I always wonder how anybody could trust this man with their money. Someone who does a poor job taking care of himself or who drives a car worth twenty bucks is not a person who I'd ask for help investing. I'd rather have that go-getter who looks like he makes so much dough that he has money to burn. My guy would drive the top-of-the-line whatever and wear only the best clothes. His appearance would be that of someone I would wish to be.

Read the Ads

Buy a weekend newspaper and take note of the advertisements. Do the ads look competitive for the marketplace? Is there an overabundance of fine print? Are they overly misleading? Are there deep discounts? This is important to help you try to understand what may be happening with the product.

If you feel that an advertisement may be too misleading for your tastes, then do not apply there. You will not change the management. The way they conduct business is evident within their ads. Read them. Look into them. What is it you see?

Perhaps the ads are not aggressive enough for you. Maybe you feel they should give a bit more money or information. If you have concerns with what they are doing before you step in the door then do not bother.

What an advertisement says to you may be your first insight into how the product is selling within the market place and who is buying the product. Both of these concerns are very important. What do you have that would further the sales of the product? Are you "the boy next door" and the product sells to your neighbors? Are you going to sell to "first-time buyers" yet you happen to be a mature female salesperson? Is there an ethnic concern? Do they advertise that they speak a specific language which you happen to know fluently?

Think about the dealerships in your area that are not represented in the paper at all. Would one of these dealerships be better suited for you?

Ask yourself these questions while you comb through the paper. Do not put all your weight in your answers. Believe in your hunches.

Shop Where You're Thinking of Selling

Begin by shopping potential dealerships. Don't go pissing anybody off or wasting anyone's time. You don't want to be remembered if you decide to work at this place. "Great. This is the guy that stroked me for hours on a Saturday. I missed my bonus because of him...etc."

Visit when it's slow. Weekdays, midday, Tuesday through Thursday is usually good. See how long it takes for someone to offer to help you. What do they say? Does it sound canned? Can you see yourself saying what they're saying?

Take a walk around the lot. Look for trash, both on the cars and in the bushes. Is the place clean enough for you to work with? Are the cars presented well? Are there a lot of cars jammed together with door dings abundant? Good to know. Maybe they have an overstocking problem and the manager will be blowing out the merchandise, not caring if you make a buck or not. Maybe the management doesn't order the right vehicles with the right equipment. Crank windows are out. All cars should have air conditioning nowadays. It's the 21st century!

Do the other salespeople look happy? The one talking to you. Is he or she smiling or spending time looking over his or her shoulder every couple minutes? Are they afraid of someone? Are they preoccupied with wondering if their boss is watching? If they seem afraid, why do you think they are?

Shop by Phone

Perhaps the single most common concern overlooked in dealerships today is their phone systems. Since there is no real way to gauge a control factor regarding incoming phone calls for various staffing or monetary reasons, the true amount in dollars that is lost due to poor phone control is unknown. We will discuss in a later chapter ("Your Role and Responsibilities") what you can do to help and where you are responsible.

Before heading into your dealership of choice use that newspaper and give them a few phone calls. See how many times the phone rings before someone picks up. Is the person on the other end a receptionist or does an answering machine pick up? Is your call efficiently routed to the sales floor or are you spending your time lost on "permanent ignore?"

When you get a salesperson on the phone ask about a vehicle in the advertisement. Listen to the response given by the sales associate. Does this person sound as if he knows what he's talking about? They should know the advertised vehicles like the sound of their own names. If they do not seem to know anything you should wonder if the management has done their part in informing the sales staff of what may be called on. Is there a communication problem in the store between management and floor sales personnel? True, not all salespeople will spend the time to get to know the vehicles or listen to the management's encouragement to touch them, so a few calls separated by a few minutes or hours to ensure different results should be attempted.

A salesperson who handles the phone poorly could increase your opportunities within the store. You may be able to take advantage of their weaknesses. Some salespeople are very good at following others around and feeding off of their droppings.

Many salespeople will play dumb or follow a script that allows them to track the customer with name and number at the very least. If this is the case it will be obvious after repeated calls. Scripts can be a persuasive tool to get customers in if used correctly and followed up on. We will discuss a workable model in the "Phone Skills" chapter.

Shop by Internet

Like it or not, the dealerships' Internet Departments are quickly taking the place of their Fleet Departments for true retail purchases. Internet business is growing at a staggering rate and those responsible for managing it have their commissions and pay structure evolving with it and often changing monthly.

Internet Department managers may do almost anything to get the business they can. In many stores the retail floor salesperson and Internet Manager are working the same customers, who pit the two departments against each other in an attempt to get the "best deal." By shopping the Internet you will discover some of the soap opera antics that may be present, and which you could become a part of if you choose to work at that dealership.

First you will find out if the dealership has an Internet presence. This is important since so many people are trying to get information via the Internet and are finding themselves stuck in the Internet currents, pulling them toward some advertisement or another to get a price for that vehicle they are reading specs on. If your dealership isn't part of the undertow it will surely be in the future, if it has a future.

Second: If the Internet Department is quoting prices without attempting to bring you into the dealership then you will find your retail department front end gross profit (what you are paid on) reflects a lower than average amount.

Think about your potential customer, whom you have spent a day or so with during his lunch break midweek. He goes online prior to his appointment with you on a Saturday morning. He's sitting with his coffee and newspaper, reading the ads. He pulls up your dealership and checks the inventory for the availability of a specific vehicle. He finds it! Little does he know that vehicle just arrived and is buried in the service department with a transmission problem. He gets his price and drives in. When he arrives he asks you about this specific vehicle without telling you that he found it online. You know it exists in the service department because you've seen it, being a professional and having walked back there the day prior. You also know that your manager has told you to stay out of the back end and that you cannot sell that specific car until it is okayed by the manufacturer as being repaired. You want to avoid the hassles. You tell your customer it doesn't exist. He thinks you're a liar but doesn't mention it. Let's say you land on another vehicle with a little more equipment. It's something he'll take "if the deal is good." You present the deal and he whips out an internet bid for pennies. Having fun yet?

Just something to think about when you're deciding where to work.

Shop in Person

The weekend is usually the busiest time for the sales floor. You should arrive midday and see what amount of coverage they have. Are salespeople standing around waiting for customers? If so, how many of them are standing? Do they look like they wished they were somewhere else? Are they smiling? Do they look like they're "hungry?" Maybe they're "fat" with money or just plain lazy. Could you run circles around them? Do they look like ex-cons or professionals? Could you see yourself buying a car from them or working with them?

You can leave and return later if you think you might have come at the wrong time. Timing is everything, they say. This is true. Come back when you feel they'll be busy. People are much like machines. When they're well greased and each individual is doing his part of the work, you may see how their team is. Do they really hum?

Let the salespeople approach you. See how the person responds to you. See what they say and how happy they seem. Ask them what you can expect to pay for a vehicle you pick out. See what their response is. Is this response canned? If it seems that way it may be, though that is not a bad thing unless it's a very foolish response that you feel wouldn't work for you.

When you drive by the dealership, is there more than one way to enter it? If so, that means there is more than one way for customers to leave. If you can limit the customers' escape routes you will find it easier to control when they leave.

Is there ample parking for customers? If you couldn't find a parking space, what makes you think your customers will be able to? I worked in an auto mall where the parking problem was an epidemic. The owner wanted me to offer ideas on how to increase sales. I had employees' vehicles towed.

What do you see? Are there twenty guys standing in a line-up waiting out front? How would your customers feel trying to approach? What would that sort of line-up do to the way you approached the customer? It can be a good thing if handled correctly. Would you stand out or blend in?

Does the dealership appear clean and inviting? If nobody cares about the place they work it will show in the gutters, streets, and planters surrounding the facility. Cigarette butts thrown carelessly about and fast food wrappers hidden in the wheel wells of vehicles talk of unproductive employees and stale inventory hanging around too long.

The answers to these questions are not as important as what you feel about the answers. The main questions are "Would you shop at this dealership?" and "Why?" These answers are considerably more important. Write them down once you find a place you would like to apply to work for. You'll need to review them later.

Applying for Your New Role

○ ○

"It's good to know where the bear is in the forest before you go hiking."

—_Richard Ziegler_

Egos

Now that you've found a place to apply where you feel you will be successful, it's time to get hired. In this section we will cover what you should wear, the egos you will meet, selling yourself in the interview and beforehand, as well as what questions you should ask before accepting your new role.

It is best to recognize that you will be entering a territory where those who sell the most cars are constantly having their heads inflated. Upper management often builds confidence in heavily exaggerated amounts, which helps make these strong closers stronger. It is typically the strongest closers who are promoted throughout the ranks and they maintain the top positions in many stores. These are the people who you will be interviewing with.

Some stores may even have you complete an interview with their best salespeople or team leaders to get the buy in from these top producers. It is this buy in, where the okay comes from the person who may have the hardest time with new competition, which allows upper management the opportunity to see if their sales floor may be upset by hiring you.

Know your rank in the food chain. As the green pea you are considerably more expendable than anyone else on the sales floor. It is easier not to hire you to begin with than to allow turmoil from clashing personalities. Typically this upheaval causes excessive chatter on the sales floor and cuts down on positive attitudes and working deals. It often leads to top producers dropping ultimatums in management's lap, which everyone knows about and is waiting with baited breath to see how the ultimatum will be addressed.

One of my mentors in the car business stated once that he would like some time to think about what had been posed to him when he had been delivered such a concern. The person making this statement to him continued to prod. He quipped back that if he had to make a quick decision without the opportunity to review the facts then the decision would not be favorable.

Nobody wants to be put in a situation that forces action. We would prefer to keep status quo over being babysitters for the training period that follows hiring fresh blood.

Keep this in mind when you call upon the management to apply for your new role. Be a spectator and a student. Listen to the hum on the floor while you wait to be interviewed. Watch what the other salespeople are doing around you. Are they pretending to conduct business indoors, within earshot or sight of you? If they are not with a customer they have no business inside. Most likely they are marking their territory while you are present.

Dress for Success

Dress like you made it. Fake it until you do. People enjoy buying from successful people. They enjoy surrounding themselves with successful people. When you buy a car there is some little thing inside you that says, "I want to be a success." Buying a new car can give a person that feeling. Let them feel that way by your lead.

You want to wear clean, pressed clothes. Try non-offensive clothing that is businesslike and appropriate for the area you chose to sell in. If you work in a primarily older community they may feel more comfortable if you were to wear dress slacks with a white shirt and tie. If you work in a progressive community that may be more liberal, wear colored shirts, maybe polo shirts or dress shirts without a tie. Whatever the majority of those you're going to help wear, you will wear.

Try not to go overboard for anything other than the interview. While working as a closer one of my salesmen invited me into his office to shut a deal. I was wearing an Armani suit my wife had given me as an anniversary present. When he introduced his customer to me the customer stood up, checked me out from head to toe, and walked away. As my salesperson tried stopping the customer from leaving the customer said, "See that guy? He'll kill me. I'm not buying from him, or you," and he left.

I put that suit away for special occasions like applying for a new position and brought down my wardrobe.

Sell Yourself

Know what you bring to the party. You have something that others do not. What is it? What makes you think you can sell cars? Be prepared to tell them why they should hire you. They need to know that the time that they are about to spend with you in training is going to be fruitful. Nobody wants to spend a few days of their life holding your hand and showing you the ropes only to find out that you've had a change of heart or cannot handle some facet of the position.

Even if you sold cars before, they will want to "train you" to their sales processes. Act like you have nothing to learn and you won't have the chance to learn anything other than where the door is. Appear and state your enthusiasm to work with their team and learn from them and you will find them welcoming you with open arms.

"You can't teach an old dog new tricks." Cliches, old quotes, and stereotypes all have their place in our world. Once again, they exist because they're true. At least they have held their own at some point in history. As with any rule, there are exceptions. You can always be that exception if you do not like the stereotype that attempts to define you or something about a part of you. However, if you are an "old dog" you should do everything in your power to overcompensate and keep quotes like this one off the lips and out of the minds of people who are around you.

Product Knowledge

What do you know? This business isn't as much about cars as it is about people. It is important to know what features the vehicles have and how they may benefit the customers. Yet the customer's needs and expectations change swifter than vehicle models and their options. You don't need to get into what you know about cars within your interview. If this is a strong suit of yours, then just mention it and get off of it. Don't waste your interviewer's time with your rambling.

I know a particular salesperson who walked into my life as a "green pea." He applied as one at least. He'd come from another state where he had sold as a front line sales person at the same dealership for over five years. He was a very competent professional yet for some reason he hadn't been offered an opportunity to advance in his career. He later told me that he believed there was some animosity between himself and the management in that store. The management wouldn't fire him because his sales numbers were always better than the average guy. They would not promote him either. He felt that he could get a fresh start in a completely different place.

I was not in charge of hiring at the time. He was hired by my manager who immediately took him under his wing, while at the same time accepting credit for how quickly he learned. He was a manager's dream. He was a natural. He was promoted quickly and now runs a nearby dealership.

What he did was brilliant. He knew that the interviewer wanted to "discover" him. The interviewer wanted to take credit for being able to train someone so competent. Because of this the interviewer surely overlooked some obvious signs that he already knew what he was doing. At the same time he did a fine job of disclosing nothing and keeping his past a secret. He was protected by his "trainer" and took advantage of his opportunities when he had them. He kept quiet when he needed to and spoke when encouraged to do so. What did he know?

The Phone Inquiry

I don't believe that a phone call is a good way to begin showing that you're interested in working for someone. If you were truly interested you would visit them personally and tell them so. In person you have a good chance of making a memorable impression.

However, if you decide to call first to schedule an interview then so be it. Ask for the general sales manager. He's the guy to talk to. If you ask for a manager you may end up talking to any number of salespeople who feel it is their job to come between all phone call inquiries and their managers. They may and will have their own agendas if they're worth their salt.

Don't ask if they are hiring new salespeople or if they have any openings. None of that matters. In this business, if you're better than what they have then they always have an opening. You have to be what they want. Make your statement strong. Keep your words concise and simple. Say, "I want to work for you. When should I come to see you for an interview?"

There isn't a general sales manager I know that has the time to stop what he is doing and start a game of twenty questions over the phone. Especially when the person on the other end of the call is so sure and so willing to schedule an appointment with such tenacity and dedication and no discussion whatsoever.

Whatever you do, do not get off the phone without making the appointment. If you are told to call back later to speak to someone else then ask when that person will be there and set an appointment to show up at the dealership at that time. If they won't set an appointment with you, then set one yourself and tell them when you will be there. Encourage them to let the general sales manager know that you will be coming.

The Interview

On interview day arrive early and walk the lot. Get a feel for the lay of the land. Is the lot big enough for you to spend the next few years walking around? You're going to be out there for hours. Is there any protection from the elements whether it's a hot or rainy day?

How does the place look? If the place is well kept there is either pride or money as a motivation, as well as a financier. The owner is proud of his business. The employees are happy to be working there. Or they make very good money and the owner spends tons like water. In either case everyone is happy. On the contrary, the place might look rundown. Trash and cigarette butts are everywhere. The shrubs are twigs buried in this garbage. The showroom is dirty. Cars are all over the place and poorly parked or kept.

How are the employees? Are they smiling and friendly? Listen to them long enough and you'll know. You'll hear something. Someone griping about something internal. It's a small world on that lot. People talk. You listen and you'll hear.

Take a seat in the service department customer lounge. Read a magazine and wait for a few minutes. Maybe have your oil changed. Listen to the buzz and see how they treat customers in service. A great service department is an incredible asset on the sales floor and in the closing room.

Approach the receptionist or sales manager a few minutes earlier than your appointment was set for. Be polite. Have a good smile and pleasant tone in your voice. Offer a handshake while you greet them and say your name like they should know who you are.

Remember this is your shot as well as theirs. This is the chance to meet them and to see how they respond to you. You get to interview *them* in the way that you answer questions. Pay attention to the fact that you get to ask a few too. But wait until they are done with their questions before you begin yours. They'll invite you to ask if they intend to hire you.

There are dynamics that happen in each relationship. Meet as many people you can. Preferably everyone you're most likely going to be answering to. Every desk manager that you will need to know and get numbers from should be someone you meet to understand how they respond to you. Shake hands and always state your name with great eye contact. How do they respond to you? Can you trust them? Can you learn from them? Would you feel good working for them?

I interviewed a guy for a position who answered a series of questions and really seemed to interview me very strongly with the exception of being a little angry when he went off on a tangent about the size of his nose. I hadn't noticed. He seemed to think it was a problem. His nose wasn't a problem that would keep me from employing him.

I believe in the tool box theory. Everybody has a chance with me. I need as many tools as I can find. Diversity within my sales team is crucial to the team's success. When I need a hammer I have one. If I need someone who is slow and methodical he is there. The boy next door. The grandson. The grandmother. Even the guy with the "big nose" has a position on my sales floor. By keeping them all in my tool box I can do any job.

I did not offer him a job. I asked him if my store was a place he'd like to work if offered the opportunity. He looked away and crossed his arms. He said something about getting a signing bonus that another dealership happened to offer him. I've never given anyone an up-front bonus that has paid off. Why would anybody give money to someone who is coming to them to work on commission? If they're so good why don't they earn it? That's the beauty of commission. You get what you are worth. No signing bonus.

Well, it didn't really matter. I was feeling like I was being lied to. He then offered the name of the store that was doing this. I happen to know the owner of that store personally. I worked for him once and we play poker together every now and then. He doesn't offer signing bonuses.

"This guy is a liar," I thought as he went on about "if I decide to work here I'll let you know."

I didn't entertain hiring him once I felt this way. I quickly stated that he should go look at the places higher on his list and that I'd hate to hold him back. We wouldn't get along well. I have a program and he is "already trained." No problem. He left.

The next day he calls me: "Okay. I've decided to work for you."

"Who's this?" I asked.

"Bobbie."

"Bobbie who?"

"I applied with you yesterday. I'm ready. I'm going to work for you."

"Oh. I'm sorry. We've decided not to hire you. We're going with someone else. A green-pea."

I could see that we were are already clashing.

"You're prejudiced. I'm going to the labor board."

"Prejudiced?! Against what?"

Yada Yada Yada…

Click!

What didn't he understand? We weren't clicking from the start. Why would he lie to me and then think that I wouldn't know?

What is it I am prejudiced against? If anything, I can admit to being somewhat prejudiced in favor of hiring "geeks" like Bobbie.

Geeks know what it is like to be told "no" repeatedly throughout their lives. They're already used to rejection. They understand fantasy as well as wants and needs better than any other section of the population. They've been beaten up and turned down. Their tenacity is second to none. They've watched the popular people well enough to understand what makes them tick. They have become unusually smart out of sheer social boredom. They are always my first choice.

If you get in a battle or feel uncomfortable in any way, leave. Don't stay there. You're not going to make any money if one of the managers doesn't like you. When that person is running the show you'll be getting very little or negative attention. It doesn't have to swing from the start but you do have to feel you could drink a beer or have dinner with these guys. You're going to want to be able to have a conversation with them. You'll be spending more time with them than your wife, children, mother, girlfriend, whomever. You're going to know everything about them and they will learn about you. You'll be sharing stories over and again until they tell you to shut up. The time will come if you're there long enough.

This is the time to walk away before you start. Once you start you cannot quit in the first 90 days. You owe it yourself and to them. Hang in there. Keep trying. You'll know when it's not working once you know what working is. Learn everything you can for 90 days. See how many of the people you can spin during that time. Or leave now and do not waste anybody's time.

What You Can Ask

Wait until they have completed their interview of you. They will ask you if you have any questions. It's important to ask all the questions you want. Just don't ask questions that they have already answered at some point during the interview. Just because you weren't paying attention doesn't mean they have to repeat themselves. Pay attention.

If they seem preoccupied with their daily routine, show patience. Allow them to go about their business if they need to. Many stores are run with too few decision-makers, or they do not empower their people to make basic decisions. I would not encourage anybody to work in this type of store. However, if this is their only flaw it could be an asset for someone who has natural abilities when the dealership typically promotes from within. A constant interference could mean that you are talking to the right person.

Pay Plans, Demos, & Bonus Stores

Every store is different. Some offer demonstrator vehicles for you to drive. Some have larger than average percentage pay outs relative to commission-able gross. Some stores are designed to pay the majority of your monies out in bonuses for performance and longevity. Some stores have ridiculously high "packs." Whatever the case you need to know that if it sounds to good to be true then it usually is.

This book has a complete glossary of useful terms that you may turn to from time to time. Read them completely when you are able. I will share those relevant to your pay and give an example of typical calculation for you to use as a benchmark.

Front End Profit:	The amount of money from actual selling price minus invoice and dealer pack plus any trade in allowance adjustment.
Pack:	The amount that dealers set to hold in reserve for themselves. It comes out of the profit prior to calculating Front End Gross.
Trade Allowance:	An amount given the customer for their trade-in.
Actual Cash Value:	The actual value the customer's trade-in is worth. This may differ from what the customer gets. Anytime it does there is either monies added to or taken from the front end profit prior to calculating commission-able gross.
Example:	If the selling price of the vehicle is $20,000 and the invoice is $19,000 you would have $1,000 front end profit to begin with. Many dealers "pack" the first $500 from invoice so you would need to subtract that from the $1,000 you began with, leaving you with $500. Let's say that the customer had a trade-in that was worth $10,000 and you gave the customer $8,000 for it. There would be an additional $2,000 to add to the $500 you had, for a total of $2,500 Front End Profit.

Keep in mind that all dealerships may have different pay outs of percentage of commission-able gross. The effectual pay out can be altered by increasing or decreasing packs and adding unit and retroactive percentage bonuses. Let's take the above example with two different pay plans and see what the outcome regarding effectual percentage pay out is.

Option A:	Let's pay you 20% of the $2,500 with a bonus of $100 for maintaining a gross over $2,000 and an incremental unit bonus (if you sell more than 15 units in the

month) of an additional 5% retroactive. Your commission would be $600 with an effectual percentage of 20% if you don't hit the incremental unit objective. However, if you do achieve the incremental unit objective, your commission goes to $725 and your effectual percentage becomes 24%.

Option B: In this option we will make two changes. Your percentage will be 30% and the store will have a $1,000 pack with no bonuses. Commission-able gross becomes $2,000. Your Commission would be $600. Your effectual percentage would be 20%.

As you can see your pay is subjective. If you really want to know how fair the pay is then ask these few questions: What are the other sales professionals getting paid? How long have they been working there? What did the top producer and the bottom feeder make last year? Is there a training plan and must you pay for it? Do they allow you a demonstrator vehicle to drive? Do they offer and contribute to a 401K or some other tax deferred investment plan? Do they pay your medical insurance?

Training Programs

Our business is constantly changing. The vehicles change to meet the customers needs. The financing and leasing programs adjust to economic conditions which, as we have seen, could and will change overnight. The customers change by researching information online and we must adapt to them being increasingly more educated and misinformed. We must train constantly.

The manufacturers encourage product as well as specialized training. It's usually paid for by the dealership. I've heard of dealers who charge you if they go out of their way to set up the training and you do not show. I'm not sure how I feel about that. I don't understand why a professional salesperson would not attend free training.

Some dealerships will pay for you to hone your skills at various offsite training schools which are quite costly but well worth their weight. I have a reference section at the back of this book containing those that I would recommend. If the dealer does pay for this type of training then I applaud that dealer. Take advantage of all that you can get. Ask what training will be available for you and who will pay for it.

I don't remember the first time nor can I tell you how many times I've heard or shared this story. It's been around for as long as I have been in the business and I have no idea who takes credit for first telling it. But I know its lesson to be true.

There were two lumberjacks in the finals of a competition to see who was the best lumberjack in the world. An old-timer, who had been known to cut through a dozen trees in less than an hour and a newcomer, of whom little was known. They both stood with their axes in hand as the starting bell rang. People watched while wood chips flew and they seemed to be in equal positions as their first trees fell. The old-timer stepped to his second tree as the newcomer walked off into the neighboring forest to the bewilderment of everyone who watched. Meanwhile the old-timer finished off his second tree and was halfway through his third when the newcomer returned, making short work of catching up with and passing his competition. A bit frustrated, the old-timer attempted to work harder, trying to catch up. He was pleased to see that the newcomer again walked away into the neighboring forest, so he was able to make up time and pass through his seventh tree. When the newcomer returned he was nearly two trees behind and the spectators were mumbling about how bleak his chances of winning looked. The old-timer was slowing now, beginning to fatigue while the newcomer once again quickly dropped a few more trees and, while barely breaking a sweat, passed the old-timer once more to become victorious, to the amazement of all. Afterwards, when the newcomer was being interviewed and asked why he kept walking off into the forest every so often, he answered, "To sharpen my axe."

Preparation is the key to success. We must train daily and work smart instead of hard. We should practice and then practice again. Whether it's on our own or in a formal seminar with others, we have to put the time aside to sharpen our axes. And if your dealer principal pays for it, then it's even sweeter.

PART II
Knowing Who is Selling

o o o o o o o o o o o o o o o o o o o o o o o o o o o o o o o o o o o

"In every interaction there is a buyer and a seller."

—*Scott Douglas*

Verbal vs. Non-Verbal Communication

There truly are three sides to every story. Their side. Our side. The truth. But within each of these sides we are shown a bit of the other. In every positive situation there exists the possibility of us being hurt. We naturally defend ourselves by allowing that third side to help barricade us. The truth. We must look for it. Without it there could be no lie. Without the two of them there can be no reason for a story.

Think of the senses we have and how each one helps us through our daily routines. They have become commonplace and we take them for granted. The fact that we can see is enough for us to forget to look. We can hear so we allow ourselves not to listen too closely to what others might be saying, afraid of what it may be about. We can smell and the scents we have become accustomed to are not always pleasant. Perhaps we choose to ignore a few of them. We can taste and there is nothing worth tasting that we do not readily put upon our lips, already salivating in anticipation. We can definitely feel and as we age we become less likely to do so, keeping ourselves from the pains associated with any possibility of getting too close.

Three sides to everything; ours, theirs, the truth. The story exists somewhere within each of them. It is only partially told in words. The rest comes from the tones and trembles in voice as well as movements and gestures surrounding these words. If a picture is worth a thousand words, then why not take a look?

I cannot give you a road map to what every gesture may mean. The possibilities are as infinite as the gestures themselves. I can only encourage you to be mindful and remain aware. Being slightly more aware than you are now is an improvement that can make a world of difference. By reminding yourself to pay attention to what is being said you will have a distinct advantage in understanding your customer as well as your coworkers. If you can tell when others are lying it will be easier to believe them when they are telling the truth.

Believe in your gut. Your first reaction is usually right. Whether it's a reaction to what is being said or to some pattern that appears random in action, your gut will inform you of how to respond. Shoot from the hip. Take time to question yourself later. Trust in your own reaction.

I use a few basic rules to know when I am being lied to. If I ask a yes or no question and am offered much alliteration in lieu of the standard response, then there is a damn good chance that I'm being lied to. If I get a story before an answer to any question I think "lie." If the person refrains from eye contact or plays with his face in any way while answering or thinking of answering a question of mine then I feel he is lying.

With this said there is also the other side of the equation to ponder. If I'm dealing with another person and our agendas don't mix well, I sometimes allow for poor eye contact on my part to get them a bit off center. They have within them the same intuitive piece that says deep down inside, "This guy is lying." I allow them their chance to be told by this piece of them and then I respond with full eye contact and well worded conviction. This and a good handshake will usually throw them off. They'll believe anything they are told once they buy in to their own intuitions.

So what does this have to do with selling cars? If you know where the road is going before you turn the wheel, then you will have no trepidation in driving.

Human Behavior & Forming Habits

What habits do you have? Every day you do what in what order? Are your habits structured consciously until they reach the point of a habit? Like going to the same gas station every day for a pack of smokes or an energy drink? Stopping at the same coffee house on the way into the office? Driving the same back road even though it takes an extra ten minutes to get where your going, just to better prepare your mind for the day?

We find ourselves often using deliberate motions throughout our day like a security blanket. Perhaps we feel that if we don't have that coffee, stop for that muffin, or travel that road that we will fail. We'll feel uneasy and our day will be off. Something about us will be out of focus. Not right. Let's use this behavioral trait which we all share to some degree to form lasting positive habits.

The habit of arriving early at the dealership every day is a good place to start. I believe that a salesperson should be at the office a minimum of thirty minutes prior to going on duty. This is the time he can use to organize his daily schedule. Review what he will need help with from his manager and prepare to set aside a few minutes to discuss the daily concerns prior to his floor time.

This is a great time to walk the inventory, especially if he's been off from work for a day or two. Vehicles come in daily. Who knows what might have become available? Maybe a deal you were working prior can be made now because of the right vehicle showing up. Check your used vehicle inventory especially. Chat with the Used Car Manager about what gems he has out there. He'll love you for it and he'll give you the spoons when they occur.

Check your mailbox for any business that should be addressed prior to starting your shift. Upper management or a co-worker may have left valuable information about a deal or customer follow-up that will need some attention prior to your floor time.

If you're the kind of person that needs a bagel and a cup of coffee and a crap prior to taking a customer for a ride, then you should do this now. Get it done before your manager shows up and your time begins.

Another good habit to have should begin with your manager meeting with you daily. Either one-on-one or in a group, you should have the opportunity to discuss your days' routines prior to the starting bell. You may have a slower day than your manager had planned, unaware that he needs help which may put a deal in your lap. He may be too busy to tell you about it. Take time every day to ask him what his daily plan is and tell him yours.

This is also a great time to warm up. Every star athlete does it. Stretch out prior to game time. Grab a co-worker and walk around a vehicle. Throw out objections and see what he says to overcome them. Take turns being the customer. Have fun and try to make him smile. Get a laugh or a chuckle out of someone that is bored with every one of your stories because you spend more time with him than your wife and you'll be ready to spin a looker into a buyer. Try it. Do it. Daily.

Habits can be good or bad. Let's fill our time with as many good habits as we can so that maybe some of the bad habits we have will be altogether forgotten.

Some bad habits could keep us from selling a car. I smoke on occasion. Usually the occasion is whenever I'm outside. My guys know this. Sometimes I am so busy that they walk up to my desk and flick their lighters, nod at the door, and walk away to have me follow them. They have me down. It's their only time without a customer that they get me. They don't even smoke and they always carry a lighter.

This bad habit I can do without. Sometimes I work through smoking. Forget about it all together. My customers don't. They can smell that morning cigarette on me at lunchtime. I cannot get the smell out. It won't leave. Some people cannot handle the smell. It repulses them. Hard to sell to a person who is already predisposed to trying to get away from you. Why make it any easier for them to have an excuse with your stench?

Help out others who smell. Give them or encourage them to have a breath mint. It's never wrong or embarrassing to inform another salesperson of something that will help increase his sales. If it improves his life along the way, then so be it.

There exist offensive habits of all types. One bad habit that many of us have is the habit of becoming comfortable within our workplace. This comfort relaxes us to a position of free chatter. The dialogues we share are often overheard by customers who seem to be around every corner when we least expect it.

This happens in any workplace. Think of times that you have been out and overheard other people talking within their work environments. The memories are usually of conversations with negative remarks. Either fowl or abusive language, as well as poor moral and internal issues. These memories are not conducive to drawing you back to the places or people who gave them to you. Why would you want to revisit a place that is so negative? You wouldn't, and neither would your customers.

I believe that after every customer interaction, whether a deal was consummated or the customer left, those involved should take a few moments to review what went right and what could be improved. This should happen while the acts are still fresh in everyone's mind (without it getting in the way of working fresh deals). A quick review may offer insight into how you can bring that customer back within minutes, as well as ways to overcome specific objections for future prospects. This meeting as well as any other that revolves around the customers or internal working conditions should always take place inside the main desk manager's office and beyond earshot of possible customers.

It is not encouraged to get together to talk about the customer in a degrading or insulting way. We are not here to find excuses as to why we wouldn't sell the customer a vehicle, but instead why they did not buy one.

I remember learning this from my own mistake. It was a busy weekend when I spent a couple hours trying to sell a car. I don't remember the details of the sales pitch. After the customer left I returned to the pad, where a group of salesmen waited to here what went wrong. After a lengthy, excuse-riddled story of what the customer said and my rebuttal, all but one salesman was laughing wholeheartedly. I turned to the salesperson who was not smiling or laughing. He stood stoic as if waiting for me to repeat the punch line. I asked him if he understood.

"What do you mean?" he asked. "Did you close the deal?"

"No," I chuckled.

"Then what the hell did you waste five minutes of my life for, telling a story without a happy ending? Next time talk about your victory. I can't learn from your excuses."

Competition

You may say it with me without believing it. It is true. Competition is good. It keeps us on our toes. We train harder and work smarter. I've seen salesmen work in the rain on the last day of the month, a Wednesday, staying until 1 a.m. trying to get that last unit out the door and burning gas. They're there meeting their objectives and surpassing their goals. More importantly, they are there because a co-worker has one more unit than they do and they do not want to be number two. Even if there is no monetary value.

It's a plaque that says they "were" somebody once. Once. The plaque gets older every day. It's obsolete when they get it, yet they're there. Trying to be the one with the bragging rights and getting the firewood. They wouldn't have it any other way.

This leads us to other issues. We often look for ways to sabotage our fellow workers rather than allow the race to be a good one. In this business many of us just want to win. No matter the cost. We buy points and deals from other salespeople. We find ways to "crap out" the other guys and get them off the floor so we can have the customers. We need to review this.

When I was on the sales floor I worked my customers to a point where I did not wish to see them leave and return again. I felt there was nothing left in the deals, either due to the owner dropping his drawers prior to the customers walking by or my own suggestions, made in an attempt to fish for commitments. Because of this concern I worked each and every customer back into the store on Saturday or Sunday of the upcoming weekend with the idea that "there could be no better time." I told them all that I would be very busy, yet they would get all my attention if they could show right at 1 p.m.

On the weekend I would grab my dealer plate and walk by the sales manager's desk religiously at 12:30 on both days. It appeared as if I was off on a demonstration drive with a customer while I was actually off for lunch. I'd pick up my lunch and take it around the back into our service department, which was closed on the weekends. I'd sit and eat, listening to them page me to the showroom floor. I had quite a few people return as I had "pencilled" them in. They asked for me. I was on half of those deals and no longer had to work for them.

This dealership did not have a "marriage policy." I would get half of the deals that asked for me yet the salesperson working those deals wouldn't get any of the deals I was working. I took them off the floor and I worked the new customers while they were busy working the customers I had let go on fictitious or bottom feeder numbers. It happened every weekend.

Most salespeople who play this sort of game don't realize where it hurts them. I rationalized that this was a "good" thing for one reason: the buying frenzy. I enjoyed walking my "new" customers into a showroom filled with my "old" customers and waving to each of them on my walk into my office. When someone wants to buy they don't want to be the only one buying. "Misery loves company." Remember that old cliche? True, isn't it?

Where the game I played hurts is when other salesmen decide to drop your customers. They stop taking turns from you. They refuse to work anybody you have touched. If they do work them they fill the customer's head with lies, scrambling to close a deal that was small when it walked the first time. The customers don't send their friends and I have to hear about every creak and moan of their new car for half of a dollar.

For the sake of an acceptable working environment: remember to keep the frenzy going but do not use or misuse your co-workers' time. They need to feel good about taking your deals. You want them to cover for you when you are not there. You need them to trust you, for your sake and the sake of the dealership.

Perception

In a perfect world you have no flaws and work in a dealership that believes in you. You are a valuable asset and are told so regularly. The product you sell never breaks. Customers only come to see you after the sale to shower you with gifts and drink a cup of coffee with you before you start your day.

In the real world we all have our flaws. Perception is important. Ask someone the difference between a pigeon and a dove. With the exception of the birding hobbyist, most will mumble a bit, giving various answers that they speak softly, almost as if they have no intention of you ever hearing their responses. They're ashamed of their ignorance. Answer for them. Say "perception" and watch them agree.

Sure there are real differences, as my nine-year-old boy pointed out. But hell, they look like the same bird to me and to most everybody else I have posed this question to. In this and in all selling, perception is the key.

<u>Getting and Keeping Control</u>

○ ○

"My mother was beautiful, man. When she walked into a room where she saw a vase and flowers, instead of arranging the flowers she arranged herself around them."

—Unknown

When I first started in the car business one of the first statements I heard from my manager was, "Tony, get control of your customer." It is a simple thing to say and do but, like me, I'm sure that whether you are green or an old pro you still have some questions on what it really means and exactly how to do it. I asked for direction time and again but received little organized help on the matter. If you get nothing else from this book, I know you will be better at understanding control when you finish this chapter. This alone will increase your ability to work more deals, increase your profits, and help you boost your confidence during the close.

What is Control?

Control could be a catch-all for inexperienced management personnel. They may have been trained poorly by people who were trained the same way. Their understanding of control as well as how to get it and communicate it to you may not be very good. Rather than admit their lack of ability to give proper direction they can simply make this statement and disregard you while labeling you an incompetent. Keep in mind that you can only be as competent as you are perceived to be by your teacher or as you are allowed to be by your managers. As of now that will change for you.

Control is your ability to impose your will upon others with an expected response. It comes from conditioning them via both verbal and non-verbal influence. Within any interaction everything you say and do will support where you stand within that relationship. Such are the dynamics of any relationship.

Humans are naturally social animals. We have within us certain needs. We are already conditioned by many influences in media, social circles, and family to do what is expected of us. We know our boundaries and what we are capable of achieving by what these forces define. We can say that their influences are not strong yet we would only be in denial. We continually live up to what our parents decide as roles for us. The apple doesn't fall far from the tree.

How Do You Gain Control?

Have you ever trained an animal? Maybe your dog? Your dog wants your acceptance. He wants your love and affection. He wants you to substantiate his role as he would prefer to define it. Tell him to sit when he is a puppy and he will only sit if he is bewildered by what you are saying. Tell him to sit. Show him what you mean by guiding his body. Reward him with affection when he does what you've asked. Give him positive feedback each and every time he does what you ask. He will quickly learn what to do.

The customer is controlled in the same manner, with minor exceptions. We cannot tell a customer to do anything which he is not predisposed to do or goes against his nature. We must first gain his trust and then he may do what we ask. From the onset of our relationship with the customer, we can exhibit a foundation of who we are. This will allow the customer a starting point of reference that will show stability for him. This stability does two things.

First it allows the customer to relax. Remember that he has fear and anxiety to begin with. If he no longer has to worry about you he can focus more of his energy on his other fears. This alone is comforting to him. He knows who you are. You wouldn't do anything to put him in a negative situation. He trusts you.

The stability also allows for you to get the customer involved. You can begin by asking the customer to complete certain minor tasks. Do it with a calm voice and minimal eye contact, as if these tasks are completed by everyone whom you invite to do them. Say "open like this," "touch this," "pull here," "sit here."

Show the customer what you mean while you are making these statements. Remember your dog? You had to guide him into position when you first began to train him. Give that visual guidance and watch as your customer follows.

Whenever the customer does what you encourage be sure to offer immediate reward. Give him proper eye contact, a very healthy smile, and say "good." This encouragement is exactly what he is looking for. He wants to know he is accepted.

If it's too obvious it becomes eerie. Don't be weird. Intuition will tell you when your customer may be wondering if you're crazy. Don't push too fast. You don't want them to pull away from you before you allow them to. If you push they will fight. If you lay down they will do the same.

Building any relationship takes time. Do not rush the time it takes for them to be comfortable. Keep your pace going when you feel it is right and trust in your intuition.

As the deal progresses you will be telling the customer to do other tasks. These tasks will be determined by you at intervals that you choose. Never let the customer decide when these tasks will occur. If they try to take the lead do not acknowledge immediately, and if possible change the direction they are going with some excitable use of conversation (appropriate to the step of the sale that you are in).

For instance, let's say that you are completing a walk-a-round of the vehicle. You appear to have the customer lifting and touching in the order you want. For no reason they move away from you to the opposite side of the vehicle and ask some question you could easily answer. State to them "I was just getting to that. I have something you'll appreciate to show you first." Say it with excitement. Bring them back to where you are standing. Have a reason you brought them back, no matter how silly the reason may be. Give that reason emphasis: "These are rust proof!" Then continue where you left off and pick up your pace to arrive where their question had originated. Now it's your turn to bring up the question. It's time. You are ready for it on your terms.

It is crucial to bring up the demonstration drive at this point. We will discuss it again later, yet when dealing with control issues you must understand a basic element.

Many salespeople can do what we just discussed. They have that part down naturally. Yet they themselves become more comfortable and drop their guard. They allow the customer to become their friend, thinking they're going to have an easy deal. All signs point to a simple close.

Unfortunately it is at this point when they toss the customer the keys and say, "Let's take it for a spin." They've relinquished control to their friend. It's over. Their friend will now dictate where they go and when. Most likely when they return from the drive their friend will park beside their own car and leave. If they come inside they will walk around the showroom with no direction and it will show. Why not invite your new friend to a barbecue this weekend? It's over, buddy.

Even if you turn the deal it has no meat on it. The monies are small. Your friend is not going to close for a comfortable gross profit with some hammer that walks in the door and blows you out. They're going to defend you and they're going to leave until they can talk to you again. Why not? You're their friend. You'll give them the car for free.

So what do you do? Simply stay on course. Use the control you've created to go to the next step. Keep the pace moving. You make all the decisions.

And always keep the keys! Do not hand them to the customer until you want them to have them. Think of Christmas. The gifts are under the tree for a week or so. What anticipation children have when they cannot open those packages. Children dream of what's inside and what they'll do with them. It's within these dreams that we can exaggerate "want." We are programmed at an early age with these fantasies.

You drive first. It keeps the other vehicles from being destroyed. It helps another customer's children stay alive a bit longer for their next Christmas. It maintains your control and makes the customer salivate.

Ask the customer where they'll take their new car first. Ask them who they will show it to. Allow them to talk about these occurrences. They're dreaming out loud. Feed into it. Let them visualize themselves pulling up in front of their friends' house, that family picnic or whatever. Let them take mental ownership before they ever touch the keys.

You'll pull over in a nice place. Turn the vehicle off and get out with the keys in your hand. Ask them what they think of their new car. Help them get comfortable in their new seat, adjust their mirrors, and close their door. Walk around to the passenger seat and sit down. Now you hand them their keys and say, "She's all yours."

Watch what they do. This is where the magic happens. You'll know immediately if you are truly in control. They will glow and include you in every statement they make. Allow them the opportunity to do so.

Tell them that you are going to remain quiet by choice so that they can experience their new car. If you do not do this they may think that you are that serial killer they saw on the news. "Why is he so quiet?" Remain quiet and only give direction on where to turn or answer their questions. Do not let them drive wherever they see fit. Remember, you're still in control. You're just letting them dream that they are.

When you return to the dealership you tell them where to park. You tell them to climb out. You walk up to them and ask them what they like about their new car. Then turn and walk into the showroom while saying, "Come with me." No alliteration necessary. You don't give reason for your dog to come to you. You just say "come" and he does. End of story.

Walk into the showroom and tell them to sit down in your office while showing them where that is. They will sit. They will do almost anything you tell them to. Congratulations. You have control.

Yo-Yo Training

Let's have some fun. One of the best behavioral exercises I know came from my days as a six-year-old. My neighbor was this eighty-year-old man who loved wood working in his garage. He made all sorts of strange lawn paraphernalia out of wooden celery boxes. I would stand in his driveway, next to his skill saw, and watch him for hours. He would chat about his wife between cuts. Sometimes I would wait for him to begin cutting prior to asking him a question. The saw would stop. While the sound of it lingered my voice would fade as well until both the saw blade and my lips had stopped altogether. He'd squint with one eye, and rather than ask me what I'd said he'd pretend to have heard me and smile or nod with a nice reflective statement like "you betcha."

He had trouble hearing anyway. Sometimes I'd stand on the other side of his garage and mouth jumbled words with good eye contact and lots of gestures to see what he'd do. He'd go through his routine and occasionally walk closer to me before starting his cut.

I also enjoyed walking up to him when I first arrived and standing right in his way. Maybe a foot from him. I'd stand in that space where we feel uncomfortable and pretend to be totally content. I'd stand there until he moved away and I'd follow him sometimes. I'd continue to move next to him until he'd back himself up a few times, almost entirely out of his work space.

Maybe you could call it mean. To me it was fun. He was a good friend to put up with me and I learned quite a bit later in life about wood working thanks to him. I learned more about getting people to move where I wanted them to go and how to get control of not only their actions but when they shared them. He taught me quite a bit.

Go ahead and play with your co-workers or family when you get the chance. Try speaking softly and see if they move in to hear you better. Stand in their space and see if you can back them up into a flower planter or off a porch. Don't tell them what you are doing and you'll be able to play with them whenever you want to. You may find it useful at some point in your relationship with them.

How will you use this with a customer? Let's start with every time a customer wants to walk away from you. That's when I use it.

I speak softly so they can hear I'm saying something but do not know what it is. I always speak with a smile, however. Just so when they turn to look at me they know I'm not insulting them. Once they look at me I turn my eyes away and continue to talk while walking toward a vehicle or area I want them to move to. I'll point at something while I'm softly speaking about it. They'll approach.

If I maintain eye contact when they initially hear me they will ask what I'm saying from where they are. They'll request that I speak up. I don't want this to happen. If they try to do so without eye contact I can easily pretend that I didn't hear them. They'll believe this since our distance kept them from hearing me as well.

This works well for the customer who you have just approached when they walk on the lot. They don't know you yet. You are trying to greet them and they are standoffish. They walk away from you while you talk. You typically raise your voice so they can hear and say something that gives them permission to walk around without you. I prefer to stand still, smile with my hands in front of me, lower my voice, and say, "I'll show you the best deal on the planet. Follow me."

They'll hear what they want. They'll stop every time and say, "What?" By now I've turned perpendicular to them and began walking toward the other side of the lot while talking loud enough for them to know I'm saying something. I walk so they can see my lips moving and smiling. They'll come with me. I return to the steps.

"So. You here for the big sale? It's the biggest sale we've ever had…"

PART III
The Steps to the Sale

o o o o o o o o o o o o o o o o o o o o o o o o o o o o o o o o o

"The general who makes many calculations prior to battle is most certainly at an advantage. The general who makes but little calculations will most certainly lose."

—*Sun Tzu*
The Art of War

The Ladder

Before we begin we should prepare. Preparation is crucial to our success. We prepare by understanding basics and whenever we get off course we steer back and find what we're missing by remembering the steps to the sale.

Once, who knows when, someone decided that he'd teach "the steps to the sale." The steps were defined and numbered and taught. Everyone has a different number of steps, yet no matter what the emphasis is on or what steps may be run together, they are basic and already determined. They come in an order that has not changed.

Picture yourself with a ladder. The ladder is leaning against the wall and you peer up at your goal, the top. But instead of climbing you grab the top rung and pull yourself with all your strength, toward its perch. You may be strong enough and have no problem pulling yourself up. If you manage to reach the top you will find yourself fatigued in both mind and body. You are no longer as sharp as you could be when you need to be, in the close.

This is what happens to us when we skip steps. I say "we" because it happens to us all. I find myself often looking for simpler ways to achieve my goals. It is taking these turns that we learn. Our learning is bred in failures. How many light bulbs did Thomas Edison create before he made one which worked?

The living comes within the process. The learning comes within the outcome.

If we had taken each step on that ladder we wouldn't achieve the same goal. Our true goal: reaching the top and having the energy to do so over and over without rest. We need to sell some cars. We have money to make. We cannot find ourselves spent after one customer.

Again, the steps are the process. It is within the process that living exists. It is in this life that we define ourselves. What we become is dictated by actions and reactionary behaviors which are common threads within us all. The dynamics of these threads are predictable. Only whether they are used with positive or negative intention is all we as individuals can control. The information is here for you to use. We make our own choices on how we will do just that. I encourage you to make your choices consciously.

Car Talk

Let's focus on the first side of the deal. This is where your work begins. While you build value you gain control of the customer. The first part of the deal is the foundation for what you will do later. This is where you talk cars and only cars. Money is never your concern during these stages.

It may be brought up by the customer, however, and you may need to address it. The ability to understand whether it should be addressed or not lies within what reason it is being mentioned. You can simply try to pretend you didn't hear what was being said once. Only once. Wait to see if it worked while you return to the steps.

Is the customer stating concerns based on his financial limitations? If you feel this is the case then you can bring yourself out of this problem by focusing on your steps and stating, "It sounds like you have valid concerns. Allow me to offer you every option. Let's first find the vehicle that meets your needs. I feel confident we will come to terms." Return to the steps.

Many times a customer who is only focused on price has done his shopping somewhere else. He has found his vehicle based on what another salesperson has told him. Let's assume that salesperson is slightly better than average. Though he let the customer leave, he sold a vehicle he has sitting on his lot. The vehicle is equipped a specific way and the customer has been encouraged to purchase those exact items based on his "want" for them, as they meet his "needs" (as recommended by the other salesperson).

You have a job to do. You must make a better impression than the other guy. Maybe this customer is shopping you to validate his decision to buy from the other guy. Maybe he likes the other guy so much that he doesn't want to offer him more than a fair price so he left him and will go back to see him when you give him your number. Often this customer doesn't even get a number. He walks in and becomes belligerent thanks to some subconscious defense mechanism he brings with him. This has been referred to as "having a chip on his shoulder." He wants you to get pissed off and insult him so he will be able to "show you who the boss is" when he goes back and buys from the other guy.

Do not try and insult the other salesperson's intelligence or vehicle. If you can keep from competing in an apples and oranges game, you will have a better opportunity. The odds of you having the exact vehicle on your lot are small. The customer will lie if you allow him to. Do not ask him if the vehicles are the same. He will undoubtedly say they are. The options your vehicle has omitted will be of topic. He will not mention what the other vehicle lacks and what yours has. How will this information help you?

Speak up and allow the customer to hear you: "Sir, it wouldn't be fair for me to know about my competition, their vehicles, or their prices. Allow me to demonstrate for you what will fit your needs as well as share all the numbers necessary ĩor you to make an intelligent buying decision today. I always sell customers who shop at other stores first." It sounds like you're confident. Your confidence will give weight to your numbers.

If they do not want to get into the options of your vehicle or take a demonstration drive then tell them a story. I prefer to mention the time that I bought a car with little time:

I rushed the salesperson through the sale, refusing to drive the vehicle. It was new. Good enough for me. The car had what I felt I needed as the basic options; power group, air conditioning, automatic. However, I didn't know that a specific power train combination would have been more appropriate for the uses I intended for the vehicle. I didn't allow the salesperson to find out that I might have preferred this. He never had the opportunity to inform me of its availability. I bought the wrong car and have resented the situation ever since.

I still feel badly that I look at that experience as the worst buying experience I have had. All my friends have heard about it. I won't buy that make. I won't buy from that dealership. I won't buy from that salesperson. I won't make the same mistake again. I know it's not even their fault, but I have my pride as well. I'm not going to eat crow when I can just go somewhere else and buy something else. There are too many other choices within this industry.

Relate how important it is for you to have repeat buyers as well as their friends and family. Tell them that the bad word of mouth alone is not something that is worth selling them a car. Get them to buy in to your integrity. They will accept that you are a good person and this will help you when it comes to the initial sale item: Your "self." Your transfer of conviction in you, the professional. This story works well with many situations.

It makes sense to return to the vehicle and pull the "unique" options out with an emphasis on how they will exceed his specific needs. The customer will listen more intently once you've delivered that message. If the customer goes with you then you have got him. Stay with him and return to the necessary step.

If he does not allow himself to be redirected but continues to demand a figure then stop pushing. Smile and appear as if you're listening to him. Maybe even listen. But do not reflect what he is saying. Just nod a bit and wait for him to stop talking.

It is okay for this to happen. He's marking his territory. He's afraid of what you might do to him. He's a buyer and does not want to be "taken advantage of." He's operating out of fear. It's best to recognize where he's coming from than to have no idea where to begin.

You do not have to guide this guy the entire time. You can give some ground and see what happens. There is a saying: "Give ground to get ground."

Ask the customer what he most would like to do next and see how he responds. He may look you square in the eye and ask you a direct question. He is asking for your help. You handing him the reigns may let him breathe enough, and his trust for you will increase. Basically, he'll thank you. You'll hear him sigh as he asks his question. His question is representative of him giving you back control of the deal. Take it. It's yours. Do not relinquish it again.

Return to the steps.

What is a Sale?

A sale is a transfer of conviction. Conviction in yourself, your product, and the dealership you work for. If your conviction is apparent to the customer then they will accept it for what it seems like. They will begin to buy in. You will be able to sell them anything once you sell them everything. End of story.

Let's start with yourself. You must like yourself. The day couldn't be better and you couldn't be happier doing anything other than what you are doing when your customer meets you. Let's not be transparent and giddy. Genuinely pleased will work just fine.

If you truly like yourself you will dress well. You'll be well groomed and stand with good posture. You won't be sitting around, eating fast food, and smoking (or smelling of smoke). You won't be walking with your head down, lethargically through the lot. You won't have a frown or be watching your watch.

Customers need someone to tell them what to do. They want that someone to be you. They want a well-spoken, clean, positive person to be around them when they make their decision to buy. They want someone as successful as they are or someone who appears to be as successful as they want to be.

Have conviction in yourself. Take time to treat yourself well. Eat well. Get enough sleep. Keep positive people around you. Once again, attitude is contagious. Be the person that you would want to be around.

How about your product? What is it about your product that makes it different? Why do you, the person that they like so much now, like your product? How can they be better people, like you are, by possessing this wonderful vehicle? Maybe they'll get laid if they buy it. Maybe their family will have peace of mind. Your product must meet or exceed your needs and theirs so well that they *must* have it. They cannot buy anything but this wonderful product that you tell them to buy.

Sell them the fantasy that you and they could be driving around in your own little club of two. Going on vacations to places only people like you go. Successful people. Happy people. People who drive these wonderful cars that are purchased from such a wonderful person.

Once they buy their happy little vehicles and strangely perfect life they'll need a place to come when either of them break down. If they need to have their oil changed, get warranty work, or buy another vehicle they'll need to know that your dealership, and you, will be around to help them. When they are told in coffee circles at work that some magazine has rated the vehicle they drive as the absolute worst vehicle ever sold on the planet, they'll need to know that you are waiting for them at a dealership that stands behind you and the product you sell.

Tell them how you had decided to work at this great dealership and why it's such a wonderful place to spend seventy hours a week. Get them to believe in the dealership like you do. Take them on a tour of the dealership and point out people who make your day easier. If nobody makes your day easier, tour them anyway. Point out the service manager by pointing and loudly saying his name and title so that he hears you mentioning him to your customer. He'll smile and wave back. Watch him.

People want to know that you're going to be around. Tell them you are. It's you who they are buying. They're buying you and your convictions in the product and place. You're a good person. You wouldn't go selling a crappy car at a horrible dealership. Not you. You're too successful.

Steps

We are about to go through the steps of the sale. You should review these steps daily. Morning practice and review with your peers can prove beneficial in creating positive habits as well as engraving these steps into your head. After a month of continual practice you will be dreaming these steps.

Like robots, we learn them. We do them for a few months or until we outsell the rest of our peers and suddenly we know everything that there is. Then we rest comfortably on our past, making excuses as to why this month has been so slow. We'll pull it together next month, though. Watch out. We're going to be on fire right after we return from that family reunion that we cannot get out of.

Okay. That's not true for every one of us. But it is true for the majority of those out there in the business. The guys who did not buy this book or attend any training other than what is required of them to keep their jobs. It's as unfortunate as it is true.

The steps brought us to the place where we needed to be. A place where we led the board by a unit or two. A place where management liked us and we built an idea of who we are. The steps carried us through to this place. When we have a problem it is always in our best interest to return to these steps, as they will help us regain our footing when the climb becomes treacherous.

Step #1: The Meet & Greet

They say you only have one chance to make a good first impression. I'm sure you've heard that before at some point in your life. Once again, it's true. That first impression is the foundation of your sale. I'd like to tell you that you will be given a second chance to make a better impression, but I cannot promise anything. Some customers may allow you that opportunity out of respect or due to the fact that they need you to unlock the vehicles. You have something they feel that they need and they are prepared to use you. In doing so, you are offered a second chance to make an even greater impression. However, there is no way of knowing which customer you are getting purely by how they approach you or their reactions until you approach them.

Many salespeople choose who they will or can walk up to. Oftentimes they choose people they feel to be like them or that they can relate to in some distinct way. It's what many managers refer to as "qualifying the customer." They believe that their odds of closing a deal are greatly increased by speaking to customers that may fit a certain look or age group. For instance, they will only shake hands with couples who appear to be married, perhaps with children. Or they only talk to well dressed, older gentlemen. Perhaps they have a thing for female "one-leggers." It's a case-by-case situation.

I do believe that there is something to their qualifying. Another cliched saying explains it: "Whether you believe that the customer won't buy from you or will buy from you, you are right." The sheer act of deciding for your customer whether you have a chance to sell them or not will certainly dictate its own fate.

I say hello to everyone. I've always been the salesperson who walks through the service department looking for someone who doesn't want to buy new tires, get their brakes done, or replace a transmission. I'm that kind of customer as well. I can relate. I'd rather have something new than something re-manufactured or scratched, and I'll always pay a few bucks more for it. Maybe it's vanity. Maybe it's stupidity. Maybe it's a little bit of both. I rationalize it as "peace of mind" because the media has encouraged me to and it feels better than either of the previous choices.

I believe that every customer is going to buy. Maybe not today. But someday. If I have my way they'll all buy today. If they don't then I'll get them when they are ready. They'll remember me. I'll find a way to ensure that they do.

When I first started as a salesperson they had many rules I was to abide by. Most of the rules I wasn't told. I was just expected to know them. I let a customer go once. Directly afterwards I was told that if I let another person leave the lot without first driving them in one of our fine cars then I would have to take a car of my choice to that person's house and wait for them to drive it back to the dealership with me. If I didn't there would be some horrible retribution, up to and including possible termination from employment or death. I believed them. Why not? They'd never lied to me before.

This customer came in and I drove him in a truck. He didn't want to go for a ride but I took him anyway. I wouldn't let him leave until he went for a ride. I made it an event that I figured he wouldn't soon forget. He didn't forget. He went home after my manager spent a solid hour fruitlessly grinding him for some sort of commitment. I thought I'd never see that guy again.

Later that week I was paged into the showroom to see customers that had asked for me. I approached the customers, trying to remember their faces. I couldn't. It wasn't anybody I remembered speaking to before. It was a couple in their late fifties, and I had no idea who they were. I extended my hand as they said, "Our boy, Yada Yada, said you were awfully nice to him and we have been thinking about buying a new truck. Can you help us?" or something similar. I sold them a truck that day. Paid my rent with the commission. Ever since, I say hello to and drive everybody.

Handshake Welcome

Some people are against shaking hands with people they do not know. Or shaking hands too early before at least getting a name or a "feel" for what type of person they're dealing with. I've heard excuses about germs and carpel tunnel and hairy palm. You name it. I cannot understand it.

I want my customers to feel comfortable from the start. They need to know that I have nothing to hide and do not think they have leprosy. I'm not afraid of them and I believe that they are there to take advantage of the big sale. In this I do not want to separate myself from the other salespeople they may have met while walking up and down the street shopping for a new car. I want to be the status quo. I do not want them to remember me as the weirdo who wouldn't shake their hands.

If my customer looks at me in some strange way or turns away from me when I offer my handshake, then I disregard this and continue through with words only, welcoming the customer to the dealership. This may be a minor setback, so there's little reason to put any weight into their response.

People have unexpected and unorthodox reactions when they are operating our of fear. Remember that your customer is doing just that. He's paying little attention to what is actually going on. They say that the customer hears only about 20 percent of what's happening. Be it due to selective listening, laziness, or downright arrogance, the customer does not fully listen to us. They don't have to yet because they don't "need" us yet. We'll fix that soon enough, or it will self correct. Do not worry. Hang in there and it will turn around. First we must get by the simple hello and handshake to get into the deal. We're almost there.

Say something like, "Hello. Welcome to Big John's Auto Center. Thanks for stopping in. My names Joe Salesperson and you are?" Stick out your arm like it's a big club and wait to see if they shake your hand. No matter what they say or do, ask them, "Are you here for the absolute biggest sale we have ever had?"

There are certain things we say or do that separate us from the pack. Statements or actions that make us solely unique to the marketplace. People buy from us based on our product many times, yet there are those of us who make people buy. It is said that some people shop cars while others shop salespeople. I am the salesperson people buy from simply because of me, and not my product. I know this because I have sold many vehicles that have broken down time and again only to be towed into a service department that couldn't fix them worth a damn and may have done considerably more damage to them on occasion. Yet I am able to repeatedly overcome these obstacles and close the customer on more vehicles from me.

Why does this matter? I return to the "big sale." My mentor taught me this. He stated that most people will respond in a monotonist voice, making programmed statements out of pure laziness. We all do it. He felt I should begin separating myself from the others within the "meet and greet." I couldn't agree more. What a better time to make a difference.

When you are asked how you are doing, what is it you say? Perhaps "okay." How is it going? "Fine." What's new today? "Same shit. Different day" or "Same ole, same ole." Why do we give these responses when we could tell it our way? Let's face it: we don't want someone whom we ask this question to take twenty minutes out of our lives with some dissertation on their cat or wife or a compilation of the two. We want them to say "fine" and be done with it so we can continue walking by them and forget they ever existed. Right?

Well if we swap shoes, I do not want to be one that they can forget. I want to be remembered. Not as someone who bored the shit out of them in the wee hours of the a.m., but as someone who said something they were never expecting to hear. When someone asks me how I am doing I say, "Could never be better." When they ask me what's new I respond, "The absolute biggest sale ever!"

I do this because I was told to. I thought it was corny at first but I do as I'm told. There is a reason that my manager was working in the role he was in. He had something that made him different and he deserved the opportunity to share it with others. I had to give it a chance. What could it hurt to try? Besides, it felt better to say something that was positive than something that was programed and kept my head looking at the lines in the sidewalk.

It worked. Someone from the business office approached me the first day that I swore I'd go ahead and give it a try. He had worked at the dealership for fifteen years. It was his coffee break and he was walking around the perimeter of the dealership, smoking his billionth cigarette and making small talk with the new guy so he could get around me and get me out of his life. That's when it happened. He said, "What's going on today?" I responded, "The absolute biggest sale ever!" and his eyes widened. He wondered either what I was smoking or if it could be true. In either case, he stopped. He looked at me. Questioned. It worked. I was remembered.

Better Time to Buy

When does it happen? The best time to purchase a vehicle, that is? Ask a hundred customers when the time is right and you will undoubtedly get a hundred different responses. Most of the answers will ride piggyback on a story or two about either them or their friends and family. They'll tell you about the time that you too can get the "best deal" and exactly how they were the fortunate ones who did this.

The deal is perception. Like pigeons and doves. We need to ensure customers the opportunity to feel as though they will never get a better deal. Remember to work on their motivations. The great motivator: "fear." If they choose not to act they will never get a better deal. Make them understand that they couldn't have come at a better time.

Remember, "deal" is not "discount." Start mentioning discount and you will find yourself knocking on doors for a new place to sell, as well as a free place to live. You're not here to give money away. You're here to sell value in your vehicle and allow the customer to feel good about making a buying decision today. They may have come in to "look around." They all are just looking. We need them to know that it's okay to change their mind and go ahead and buy today. Why not? Everyone else is. The deals are that good.

Tell the customer, "You couldn't have come at a better time. We're having the absolutely biggest sale we have ever had." Does it sound corny? It is. It's also true.

The sale began when you walked into the dealership with this book under your arm. They once sold "X" amount of cars a month, until you arrived. Your abilities have increased their sales by a specific amount. As long as you work there the sale will continue. It will not stop until every vehicle has been sold and you go home indefinitely. Every day the sale becomes larger. Every minute it becomes more crucial. If you don't sell a car now you may not return to the dealership. It could be over. No more you means no more sale. Don't let it end.

Eye Contact

I cannot stress enough the importance of proper eye contact. Keep in mind that I am not saying you and the customer should always have lengthy, unblinking, tear-shedding stares into each other's eyes. I'm simply mentioning that you should be aware of what's going on with your eyes as well as the customer's. Like knowing when to remain silent, knowing when to look into a customer's eyes is important.

Knowing when to look away and allow the customer the same opportunity is equally advantageous. They may need that space to change their mind and decide to purchase. They may need it to feel as though they have succeeded in lying to you about some crazy excuse in an effort to leave. Don't rub their nose in it. Let them lie as long as you are aware they're doing it.

Think of the alpha dog in a pack of dogs. People are animals and respond very similarly. These rules are a good starting place.

People have heard through time that eye contact means sincerity. They also know that salespeople have heard and therefore train to give good eye contact. They expect it, even when you're lying. Give them the eye contact they need to emphasize what you want them to believe when you need them to believe it.

Step #2: Determining Needs & Wants Relative to Trust

Everyone has needs. It could be a need for transportation due to the fact that their old car is unreliable. If this was all that was important we would see more Yugos on the road. The mayor would drive down the street on parade in his. You would go to your class reunion on a moped. Your ex-wife would get plenty of exercise riding her bicycle. Our teenage boys would have posters of beautiful women dressed in string bikinis draped over the hood of pea soup green compact diesel station wagons.

These are behaviors that fulfill basic needs, but they do not satisfy our wants.

What is it we want in a new car? Do we want to feel successful? Will this new car make us feel important? Will we get laid if we drive it? Will we be envied when we are seen by our enemies and neighbors?

I need transportation to get to work but I want a car that will get me laid. Convince me that I will get laid on the way to work and you will get my business.

As salespeople it is our job to give them the minnow and have them feel like it's a shark. Somebody wanted the Gremlin when it was first released. We must fulfill customers' needs as well as their wants. Understand what they are for each customer and know when to use them and you will have control over the deal.

There are many roads to take to do this. They all begin with asking directions. Maps can guide you but no map shows when a road is under construction or traffic conditions are intolerable. They are a basic reference.

We will ask for help from the customer. He has the information that you need in order to begin putting your route together. Let him tell you as much as he is willing to share and you will be armed with many useful detours when the time permits, or demands your action.

We cannot ask a customer for information until we are trusted by him. Will they trust us simply because of who we are or the fact that we know the vehicles and the terrain? Absolutely not.

Even referrals from our past customers, friends, or family members do not trust us. We are salespeople. Referrals know that. We cannot take anything for granted. Even they have unrealistic expectations.

Ask anyone about their last car purchase experience. They will have stories about every specific aspect. They will remember everything that had happened to them and each nuance of the deal. Their memory of the event is phenomenal. How could they be so sharp?

Ask them to speak about the financial arrangements and it becomes even more impressive. They purchased a thirty thousand dollar automobile for twenty thousand dollars, including tax, title, and tags. Their five-hundred dollar sled they traded in was worth five grand. Their down payment was nothing. Their monthly payment of $549 becomes $500. The number of years their loan is due drops in years. Do you think that they share this information with their friends before they send them to see you?

Though we have our foot in the door with them we still must gain their trust before we can exploit it. We need to be in a position where others have made their own choices to listen to us rather than them being impressionable enough to come visit us. After all, why is this customer here? Is it because they like their friend or because their friend received such a wonderful deal?

How do we gain that trust when we first meet a person? The answer is in the question. It is in the meeting that the trust blossoms.

Imagine yourself as a single man. You meet an attractive person who could remedy your lack of companionship. Do you approach her and ask straightaway for intimacy? You may be the guy who does. What if she says yes? One out of ten might. Is this the type of person you want to spend a night with? There is a reason that "hard to get" is an expression. It works. What if she slaps you instead? You must start over with someone else. Your opportunity has passed.

Instead you sit beside her or across the room and offer the occasional smile. You buy her a drink if she drinks. You ask her to dance if there is music. You ask why she is there. You listen. You ask what she does for a living. You listen. Whenever she slows down you offer quick, reflective statements: "That sounds interesting" or "Tell me more."

She continues nonstop, filling your ears with enough of her life so that you can now pick and choose what you want to remember. You know everything about her and she smiles more with every sentence or description of how she became who she is. It doesn't take very long and she feels like you have known each other forever. You are soul mates.

You take her back to your place and do the "wonder of me" thing on the living room floor. You spin vinyl albums and drink champagne or coffee or soda pop. You stare into each other's eyes. You kiss.

You have her. One night. One year. However long it takes for one of you to become disinterested in the other. Whatever your intention, know this: she doesn't necessarily know your name.

It is in this same manner that you can gain a rapport and build the trust of anybody. You don't have to be attracted to them. You don't have to speak about yourself. You listen to them and the magic happens. It's their trust. They have to give it to you. You cannot take it. They have control of it.

Everybody wants to talk about themselves. They want others to be impressed with how smart or savvy they are. Be impressed. They want to be listened to. Listen. They want to be what they usually are not: interesting. Be interested and they will fill your head with enough information so you can choose what to remember and when to bring it up. Everyone wants to be needed. They need you, their long lost soul mate, to protect them from their fears. Go ahead. Protect them.

Interviewing the Customer

Ask the questions that will get them talking. "What are you looking for in your next car? Why?" or "Is there a specific function your new car will have to fulfill for you? Describe that function?" or "If this were a dream and you could drive anything, what vehicle would you drive? Why?" These questions and others like them get customers to begin visualizing themselves driving the car of their dreams. They see themselves behind the wheel and that picture becomes okay with them. It is a picture that they become used to and possibly absorbed in. Meanwhile, their energy is spent thinking of answers. So you can pay attention to *how* they answered, which may carry more weight.

Leave questions that only allow them to say "yes" or "no", unless they are poised for a reason. Typically, reasons to ask these types of questions arise when you are trying to illustrate control, pick up the pace, or give levity to the structure of the deal. Everyone needs a break. Letting your customer have one briefly is fine when done on your terms.

While you are collecting information you should be finding common ground. There is common ground there when you look for it. Dig deep enough into who this person is and you will find it.

I demand that all of my salespeople actually write their common ground on the customer's offer before they bring the offer to me. I want to know that the salesperson has truly done his job in learning about the customer. It is in this job that trust is built. That trust allows the salesperson to help establish the value of the features the vehicle has, and how they apply to the customer's benefit. Though this value is not specific to features, it may be rationalized there by the customer who wants to give value for the human element but has something within him that cannot do so. It is necessary for giving a reason for a deal, as well as a reason for the customer to pay more than he would normally deem appropriate to pay. Call it a tip.

Habits & Information

Once again, habits come in many shapes and sizes. Habits are our security blankets in life. We develop them even if we do not much like them.

Some people buy vehicles of a specific color. They may tell you that they do not want to be shown another red car. If you inquire as to why that is, they may say that the last eight cars they purchased were red. If this is the case, I'm showing them a red car. Maybe not initially. But sooner or later they're seeing red.

Why? Because they know how it feels to buy a red car. It is okay. They've said so eight times before. They see themselves easily in a red car wherever they go. Their friends know them in this color. There isn't much they need to change in regards to their life.

Why take these people out of their comfort zone? Why not allow them to voice their concern and then use the information you've gathered accordingly?

I once had a gentleman tell me that he was not buying. I asked him why. He said that the last six times a new vehicle was purchased in his family he was the one who purchased it. His wife had been upset six times prior. She always ended up with the hand-me-down. It was her turn to get a new car.

The only problem I could see was that his wife was nowhere to be found. She wasn't around to give her input. Since she was already familiar with him making these decisions and he was equally accustomed to digging himself out of a like situation, I saw it as only fitting to send him home in an new car. He wanted me to. He knew what he was doing. It was his comfort zone. He had gathered the energy and courage to show up to a dealership to look at cars, knowing that he was weak. He already knew how he responded to car salesmen. He let them do their jobs.

I did mine. His family experienced a seventh purchase and they continued to tell friends at parties about his crazy way of buying cars. He still is the talk of his wife's friends in knitting circles. Nothing has changed for him. He has won again. He is a winner in his new, red car.

I ask every customer what they do not like about their old car. There is more in this answer than we typically acknowledge. If we listen the customer will give us the information needed to close the deal. All information is the same. There is information which helps us make good decisions and information that keeps us from making those decisions. We only have to ask ourselves what type of information we are listening to.

What Can You Learn?

While determining the customer's needs you will be collecting more information than you may use. You don't need to reflect everything that you hear from your customer. Reflective statements from you are best used to keep the customer going. When or if they appear to be slowing down or getting off track, you may toss out a statement that shows you're paying attention and are interested. "Tell me more about that" is a good example of a reflective statement that usually keeps things flowing.

You'll surprise yourself as to what you will learn about your customer when using these types of statements correctly. They may offer personal insight that you do not want to know. Drop these topics and move on unless they allow for an opportunity to close them or build a rapport between you and them. Remember, you want them to feel comfortable enough to buy rather than leave.

Not everything you collect needs to be tossed out in front of the customer. Save it for later to share with your desk manager or use during the close. Use only what needs to be used. Be conservative.

Your co-workers and managers are in a need-to-know situation as well. You don't have to air out all the nuances of the deal when you chat with either of them. Nobody wants to hear about all the labor pains. Just show them the baby.

Step #3: Vehicle Selection & Inventory Walk

"There's an ass for every seat." Probably the first lesson I learned.

Once again we must begin by knowing that the customers are barely alive. They are using nearly every bit of energy to stand vertically and occasionally carry themselves around the car lot as we hopefully lead them. Their mouths may utter a remark now and then but rarely are they looking for a reply. They are trying to find their own vehicle. They may be picking it out by window sticker price and not paying close attention to options. Even as they ask for specific equipment you will see them stop and gawk at a vehicle (the attraction of which is the color most of the time).

It often happens that I hear a ten-minute monologue on what they "must" have in their next car and how it cannot be a certain way. Suddenly they trip over the combination of their tongue and a vehicle whose color screams "you'll get laid in me," and everything else goes out the window. You can almost hear them say, "Just send me home in that."

Be prepared for it. Watch their eyes. Listen to their breathing as it changes. That's the vehicle you're going to sell them once they come to the conclusion that you do not have that pink striped nine wheeler with fluorescent hub caps they feel every dealer should carry. You'll return to that car and sell you ass off. They'll buy it.

This is the reason we do an inventory walk with every customer. When the customer asks for a blue, 5 speed, three wheeler with leatherette interior and no air conditioning, you must react as though you just saw one yesterday. It was hidden in the back by another salesperson. You remember it because you too would enjoy driving that type of automobile, yet you had not seen one before yesterday when it had caught your eye. Take the customer for that walk. The vehicle happens to be on the farthest end of the dealership, away from where you currently stand with the customer when they request this unique dream machine.

You move with excitement. Pull your arms, waving them to you. Get them to pick up their pace. Lead, but don't ignore them. Keep your conversation rolling.

Say to them, "I guess you're here for the big sale. Right?" They'll agree as it rolls off your lips.

Make them talk by asking questions that give information. "What are you driving now? What is it you like about your current car? What don't you like? What's important for your new car to have? Would the lack of any of those items keep you from buying?"

You guide them with words and they'll answer. Listen to them. More importantly, watch them as you walk. They'll be chatting a step behind you the entire way. They'll give you what you'll need later to close them if you are patient.

Their eyes will stop on a vehicle, most likely because of its color. Remember that car. Don't stop there and start answering questions. Keep them moving. Stay in charge. You're in control, remember. That is the exact car you can come back to later. Options or not. People often impulsively buy a car because of its color.

Trucks, if they are to be used as a tool, are a different story. You'll need to understand weight and towing capacity in many cases. Do not make the mistake of selling or misrepresenting the vehicle and its ability when you're dealing with a work vehicle. You might end up losing the deal altogether, as well as your credibility.

Keep in mind that if you do not take the customers on an inventory walk you cannot keep them in the game. The longer you are with them the better chance of getting to know them and their needs. The better chance of making a deal. If we walk them, talk to them, and watch them we will make more money and close more deals. Too often salespeople decide for whatever reason that the customers are not buying because they do not have the right car. We make the car right. We're salespeople. That's our job.

Remember. Some customers shop cars but most shop salespeople. Be the one that they buy.

80% Rule

Simply stated, 80 percent of the time a customer buys something different from what they asked for. Why do you think that number is so high? You'd think that in an information age where all the figures, options, and availability information is so readily available online that customers would know what they want and how much is fair to pay when they arrive at your door. Wouldn't you?

That's the problem with many salespeople. They do think that. They're wrong...80 percent of the time.

Step #4: Presentation

Never talk money standing up. Never talk cars sitting down. Let's talk gross. It comes here in the presentation step. It is not created during the close of the deal. It's here, where we build value, that the customers' want takes over and their needs are squashed. This is where we sell them the sizzle, not the steak. This is where they pay for it.

Let's say you walk your lot and find a vehicle that will meet their needs and with which you can inflate their wants. It's parked between a series of other vehicles. Maybe it's hidden three rows deep against the curb and you must go inside to get the keys for it. What would you do?

I'd get the keys. I'd tell them to wait and leave them standing there and run for the keys. I wouldn't ask them if they wanted to wait. I wouldn't show them a vehicle that was conveniently situated where "they can get a feel for what the other car is like."

People like to believe that they are "unique." We go out of our way to be individuals. No two customers are the same. We want a vehicle that is as different as we are. The vehicle that is buried is as close to the individual, in all their glorious nature, as we can get.

After seeing you run inside to get the keys, move three other cars to show them theirs, and take the time to show you understand how important this decision they are about to make is, they will have no other choice but feel horrible if they do not buy. Let them feel this way. They want to feel special? Let them.

Your goal at this point is to pull the vehicle out and animate it. As you move other cars, un-burying the one you will be presenting, be sure to close them up and lock their doors. You do not want the customer in anything but the car you are going to show them. The car can change later. You don't have to sell that exact car. It's not about that. It's about maintaining control of what the customer experiences and deciding when they can do so. They need to become conditioned to you being the person that they go through for every concern.

Saving Face

Be aware that every step of the sale becomes the foundation for the next step. We must think ahead to keep from having to attempt to start over. If we find ourselves starting over we often show disappointment, which the customer may have as well. They too have invested time, and starting over may not be something they want to do right now. They have been given an opportunity to leave and return when "they have more time." Do not afford them this chance. Plan ahead.

Even if a customer has told me that he wants a vehicle with leather seats, a built-in DVD player, and retractable wings, I always show him a lower model to begin with.

I don't sell them the entry model. I show them one. There is a difference. I let them see what the model I'm showing them has. I do not mention options that this model does not have. If I do I may (and most likely will) be searching my lot for hours trying to find the vehicle that has that exact equipment. Always sell what you know you have.

Upon being shown the entry model the customer will mention what is important to them again. You can agree that those options are nice and let them know that you will bring them there next. It was your opportunity to let them see how nice "all the vehicles are." It is the customers' opportunity to spend the initial amount for the vehicle and then buy extra options as they move themselves up.

I sold minivans for my tenure in the business. These minivans were our bread and butter. Some people came in knowing only they wanted a minivan. The prices range from $14,999 on advertisement to $35,000. If I showed them the top of the line they would undoubtedly recall (silently, of course) that they saw one in an advertisement for $14,999. When I began to negotiate I would have difficulty in rationalizing the difference or getting much more than a $14,000 offer to begin with. If I showed them the entry vehicle they would often ask for power seats. I told a simple story that illustrates how things progress in cost:

"Yeah. I understand. My wife. She's four feet, two inches. She said, 'Honey, you can buy me a basic van. Just get me a power seat.' Well, power seats do not come in basic vans. I have to have all sorts of equipment I do not necessarily need in order to get her seat. We paid $26,000 and I'm the proud owner of a roof rack I have never used." (Pause.) "Mr. Customer, would not having that equipment keep you from buying the vehicle?"

You will find that many customers do not want to pay for the extra options. It may not be in their budget. Sure, they want all the toys. Especially after you reinforce the fact that they deserve them by showing them the model that has them.

You too must think that they deserve them. Why not? They're good people. They're your friends. However, once you get them into the box to negotiate, they are not going to ask for less vehicle. They're going to thank you and ask if they can go home to pray on it. They'll pray all right. Right after they drive a half an hour and buy a lesser model from someone they don't know. They'd rather do that than admit to you, their friend, that they cannot afford the one you had picked for them.

Always start at the bottom. Let them sell themselves up. It is easier for them to come back down when they know you believe in the entry model as well. After all, you began your presentation with it. It must be good.

Do not use the words "base," "basic," or "standard." It should have some designation from the factory. If not, call it a "value package" vehicle or be creative. It sounds better. I'm mentioning this now because you will specifically need to use it now. But it's something you should use throughout the entire process. Use it until the customer leaves in his new car.

I remember when a salesperson who was very talented had sold a few cars on a rainy day. He was running circles around the rest of the staff, who were bored and waiting inside for the rain to stop, the customers to come inside, or the day to end. His customers were leaving the registration office, smiling widely from ear to ear after signing the paperwork for their "first new car." He was there with the books in his hand, prepared to go outside and deliver their new car. He noticed the rain increasing and thought it best to just send the customers on their way. In his ignorance he stated, "Well, here. Go ahead. Take this with you. It's the owner's manual. It tells you all you need to know. Besides, your car is the base model. There really are no options to show you."

What do you think happened next? Their smiles disappeared immediately. They never left with the car. End of story.

Separate Yourself

The one thing I remember most about my teenage years in school was the fact that everybody was an individual. At least we thought we were. We wore clothes that separated us from the normal kids. We acted differently. Talked differently. We were so unique and different that there were no normal kids left. It was a world of individuals who removed themselves so far from the others that there were no others left. We had become the norm.

Is that we do as salespeople? Do we all shop at the same stores, buy the same clothes, and get our hair cut at the same barbers? Of course we do. We do this so the customers' fears are not heightened. It's a subconscious thing we do. We grew up watching television, and re-runs of "I Love Lucy" and "Bewitched" taught us exactly what a salesperson should look like.

If we are programmed with looks, then why can't we assume that we are likewise programed with expectations of other kinds? Like words and actions. We are liars because that is one of our imposed roles. It is expected of us. We dress so that we fit in with the crowd of other salespeople. How can we separate ourselves?

Each and every salesperson has his own challenge in finding what makes him unique. It is the story or thread of his life. The life song that we bring to the game which makes us interesting to others. This song is meant for others to find comfort and humanity while they spend their hard earned money.

If you think that you have no song then you are not looking deep enough. Use your imagination. Recall the events of your childhood that you remember fondly. The times you went on family vacations are useful for selling a car. The places and people who you remember meeting while taking a family trip or a day drive to visit relatives help customers relate to you. You can use these events to fill time, building rapports and easing customers into their purchases.

Do not hide your past. Open up. If you appear to have been sheltered or even average in your past, then it is difficult for others, as a majority, to relate with you when it is necessary.

If you believe that you have nothing to share or wish to keep these stories to yourself, then make up a few stories that could work for the same result. Do yourself a favor and keep the stories simple. You want them memorable and consistent. Tell the same stories enough times and even you will forget if they ever happened or not. They have become your past. That's fine.

You just do not want to contradict yourself and be caught in a lie. Give no reason for the customer to refer to you as a liar. You do not want to carry around this moniker for the remainder of your career. It is not easy to shake such a title. Take it from one who knows.

Sure you can embrace the mundane and be a boring individual without a memorable face. It is easy to say no to this sort of person. But how can you become the guy they want to buy from?

If you work in an auto mall you see how many people go from dealership to dealership collecting brochures. They often enter with hands too full to shake. What type of greeting and presentation do you think they get at the other dealerships? How can you be different?

I make my presentation an event. Clever uses of stories or funny statements can make you unforgettable. Relate the options you are presenting in a way that reflects all the parties who are there in front of you as well as those who may be at home (children, parents, friends) if you can get them to speak of them. Bring these people into the picture and the customer will visualize them sitting where they would. It's a great way to get to know their family members as well. This may be beneficial if you ever need to call their house. This is your time to shine.

A simple way to draw a line in the sand between yourself and the others is to ensure that you include your customer in the presentation. Your inclusion of the customer offers two benefits. The first we discussed as training toward control. The second helps establish value. Value that is essential to you making a living. It has a direct impact on how you will do in the closing box later on.

Value is built on showing and having the customer experience what is being shared. They say that telling isn't selling. This is true. You cannot tell a customer what they need to know. They must see it and experience it for themselves. You can merely guide them with words.

Always relate their needs and wants to your presentation. In order to do this you must know what their needs and wants are. Make a point of returning to them often, with each benefit you highlight from the feature you are touting. A safe vehicle feels safer when the customer is touching it, while you are telling a story of some past customer who just purchased their third one for their family. Let them live what you are saying.

<u>*Step #5: Demonstration Drive*</u>

Many times I've been approached by salespeople who work for me who wish to know what it is they are "doing wrong." Their sales numbers are lower than they would like, they're off pace for their monthly target, or they simply feel that they are not closing enough deals. Whatever the case, they know it when there is something missing. I don't typically have to prod them.

I ask them how many people they met in a given day and they respond with a lower number than they actually had. They don't count every person as a customer. They don't see every opportunity the same way as someone who is outside of their daily routine.

If I ask how many demonstration drives they have had they will answer correctly. They can count these. These are people that they felt were ready to deal. They have qualified these people as possibilities. Their qualifications are obviously a concern.

Why do we decide who can or may buy from us at any given time? Why not drive them all? It is not up to us to decide when someone might be a buyer. It is in our qualifying that we make mistakes. After all, if we know so much why do we ask our team members for assistance?

First and foremost, drive everybody. It is an absolute must. Consider it a job requirement. The customer has built up enough courage to step on our lot, even if only for service. They have put themselves into a position where they know that a "salesman" will most likely approach them. It is not a position that they would normally take unless there was some hint in the back of their minds that they might be interested in a change of some sort. That change could be new or used. It is a change that might be as simple as changing their wardrobe. The media is pounding them regularly in every direction that they turn. Social circles are influencing them. Their own desires to be accepted and successful keep them craving change. We have the chance to exploit it. We must allow ourselves this chance to do so.

The best example I have to reflect this is a baseball game. It takes nine innings. You have to play at least that many. You cannot score a run in the first inning and then stop play with the understanding that you have won. As each inning passes so does each step of the sale. Somebody is ahead but it isn't over until the final out. All games are won when the final batter swings the final swing of his bat.

As a salesperson, I tell myself to stay in the game. It doesn't matter where I am in the steps to the sale. I can look up at the line of other salespeople waiting for their opportunities to meet a customer while I am working with someone who I may feel is not going my way. I can see those other salespeople wishing they were working. I do not want to stop and go chat with them. I know them already. I don't have anything that important to talk to them about that cannot wait until the day is over. I'd rather stay with my customer and see if I can take him another inning. Take another swing at the ball. Try and get him to the next step.

Each step is a personal victory for me. If only for the practice and the opportunity to hear another objection. Perhaps I will hear an objection that I have never heard before. I can try new words and offer new stories. I can hear what the customer is telling me and it may have some noteworthy use in a latter deal. I have another chance to shine. When better to practice than with someone who might just happen to say "yes" at any given time? I cannot think of one moment I'd rather exist in as a salesperson.

Car sales is a numbers game. If you want to double your sales then double your demos. Drive twice as many people and you will have twice as many people to put on paper. It's just math. I didn't invent it. I just know how to do it.

I drive them all. I do not ask if they wish to take a ride. I just drive them. If they do not want to go then they will have to make a verbal or physical stand. They will have to stop me or jump from the car. They have no other choice.

If you ask someone if they would like to take a ride he can say "no." Why ask a question that will get you nowhere? Remember, the demonstration drive is another way for you to maintain control of the customer. No reason to relinquish this control by asking for permission.

<u>Your Route</u>

Now that we've decided that you will drive everybody you must have a demonstration route picked out. It is usually mapped out by the management of your dealership. If so, be sure to follow their lead and stick to their route. They have it for a reason. Usually it involves your safety.

If the store you work in allows salespeople to define their own demo route then be sure to map yours out, give a copy to your manager, and stick to the route religiously. There is usually no need to deviate from the route without first letting someone know you plan on doing so before you drive.

With the presence of cell phones, nowadays salespeople often attempt to "do the right thing" by making a quick call during the drive if they feel they must stray from their normal route because a decision maker is not present, or to stop and pick up a customer's checkbook. Most of the time the concerns are not deal breaking. If they are valid go ahead and make a decision on your own to do what you need to close the deal when you return. But be careful. Many salespeople have been known to return to a dealership alone after "making a quick stop" for one of these items. They found that they were merely a convenient taxi service for a service department customer.

Control Revisited

Remember why you drive first. Let's review the two main reasons, which we discussed in a prior section. You can never hear the same good advice too much.

Control is key. You must be the one who decides when and where the customers will have the opportunity to get behind the wheel of their new car. They must need you and go through you to have that opportunity. You are the guard of their new freedom, their new success, their new car. Always make these decisions when it is advantageous to progressing the deal.

The second reason you drive the vehicle off the lot has to do with simple mechanics. If the vehicle has not warmed up or has been sitting for a while it may run rougher than normal. This, coupled with the customer's unfamiliarity with the vehicle, may cause it to perform poorly. We need to be the one driving it so we can ensure that it warms up to a point at which we are comfortable turning the keys over. During this period, if the vehicle sputters or stalls we can easily blame ourselves and our lack of any driving skills. Anything that keeps the blame off the vehicle. Once we drive it and show there are no problems, if the customers have problems they will know it is them and not the vehicle. They will not mention the vehicle and make a better effort to drive without problems.

Talking

During the demonstration drive I do not talk. I want the customer to have every opportunity to get to know the vehicle and enjoy his or her drive. I sit back and let them take control. That is what I tell them beforehand.

I tell them this so they do not wonder why I am so quiet. They now expect me to keep quiet and are not surprised by my doing so. The dead air allows them the chance to ask questions. I answer their questions and give directions. Occasionally I throw out some quip, stating that I am excited about this feature or that. I apologize for interrupting their time and encourage them to proceed while I once again remain quiet.

I may do this a few times during the drive. Not enough to get on their nerves. Just enough for them to feel that I am genuinely pleased with the vehicle, and its options and features that are relative to their specific needs.

As well, this gives them the chance to understand and experience how anti-lock brakes, air bags, or other safety or power train options which they cannot outwardly see or touch may be beneficial to them. It lets them remember that the vehicle *has* them. It builds value in these items and the vehicle itself.

Where to Park

You need to decide where you are going to park for two different stops. Both places must offer you the opportunity to maintain control of the customer.

When you are ready to allow the customer to drive the vehicle you should have a planned stop that is away from busy traffic. The scenery around you should be considered. Do not stop in front of another dealership or in a shopping center parking lot. You do not want them to see other cars or other salespeople, or feel intimidated when they need to negotiate traffic. Keep in mind that most automobile accidents happen in parking lots.

I prefer a park setting or a ritzy neighborhood. The opportunity for the customer to walk around the car with it out in the open, where it is separated from any possible competition, is good. The vehicle looks new and may even turn the heads of others who happen by. Point it out if it occurs. Let the customers experience how the vehicle will "look" for them when they are out visiting the park or driving through their new neighborhood (now that they're successful). Let them dream.

Once they have driven the car and returned to the dealership you will need another area to park in. Do not allow the customer to park beside their car, or they will most certainly leave. We can use their old car later, when ours is not beside it.

Tell them to pull into the spot you've set aside. We refer to the spot as "the sold area." Say it firmly, with conviction: "Pull in here." As they pull in, state as if finishing your thought, "This is the sold area." Watch what they do. Some people will set the parking brake while the car is still rolling and the words are not yet dead from your lips. These people are already looking for a way out. Others will happily pull in and smile. Both situations neither mean you have nor do not have a deal. Do not put weight on either.

You will reply identically and use the same actions for both situations. Get out of the car. Do not take the keys from the customer yet. Look him straight in the eye and say, "I have something you have to see. Come with me." Turn and walk.

Do not allow them to stop you or begin with any lengthy wordy excuses. You must move them with your excitement and your actions. Remember that you trained them to listen. They will. They will come with you, if only to give you the keys that they currently have in their hands.

Many salespeople think that this is a great time to ask for a commitment. Many salespeople sell ten cars a month. Neither situation validates itself. It is a horrible time to begin fishing for some bullshit commitment.

A commitment should not be something that you have to ask for. There are ways to get the customer to give it to you when the time is right. It is never the right time to seek any commitment if you are standing up. You'll get your shot in the box. That's later. Don't miss your rung in the ladder.

If you ask a customer the standard line, "So if the money is right would you drive it home today?", you have just destroyed whatever work you have put into this person. You've told them that not only are you unsure whether they are willing to buy the car today, but you are equally unsure if the money is going to be right. You made reference to the fact that a discount is possible without even saying the "D" word. You let the customer, who had every intention of buying the car, think that he should look for a deal of some kind. You reminded them that this is the part of the deal where you're going to become "a salesperson." You woke them up from the ether with a question that demands attention. A final decision. Something they do not want to make consciously. Never wake the customer up. Let sleeping dogs lie.

Besides, what if the customer were to say, "Yes. If the money is right I will buy from you." What are they saying? They're saying, "Okay buddy. Show me how much money you're going to save me and maybe I'll buy the car." Is that really a commitment? Absolutely not.

Are you going to write this customer up anyway, no matter what they answer? I would. Unfortunately I would have trepidation in doing so. My mind would be rolling through what they had said. I'd let them go too early, without giving it a solid effort. It would be easy for them to leave since I'd already acknowledged that they had said that was their intention. Why crap myself out with this negative feedback when I need to be at my sharpest?

Instead, you have chosen to turn away from the customer while saying, "Come with me. I have something you have to see." They're going to follow you. It is time to tour.

Step #6: The Tour

We've discussed the transfer of conviction. You have had the opportunity to sell yourself and your product. Now it's time to sell your dealership. They need to know what makes your place better than any one of the other fifty thousand dealers out there in the world. What does your store have to offer them? What makes it unique? Why do you work there and why would they bring their new car to you for service?

Make a list of what your dealership has to offer. This is something you can refer to when necessary to progress the customer step-by-step into the closing offices. You do not have to mention every item that makes your dealership special line-by-line. Only mention the key points that you come to as you are walking. Leave something for the close. A magician does not use every trick he knows.

After the demo drive I walk the customer through a planned route. Usually this encompasses the service department waiting area. Most dealerships have a customer lounge, some place to buy a few snacks and watch television. Perhaps you have a service shuttle that could be of benefit while they're getting "routine maintenance" done. Typically, there is any number of employees (porters, receptionist, service appointment personnel) who happen to walk by. These are great people to point out. Mention how long they've been at the dealership and how eager they always are to help, and wave at them with a smile. These people do not get the chance to be "part of the game" very often. They will eat it up. You will look good.

Do not introduce a customer to a sales manager, desk manager, closer, or finance manager. You will want to bury your head in the concrete if you do. If you don't bury your head they will most likely do it for you. Your customer will ask them how much and what's the best rate they can get or what their trade is worth. You're a dead man. You can introduce some of these people at the right time. The right time is never when you're standing up and never when they do not have their game together.

A goal of the tour is selling your dealership. Part of that depends on how comfortable the customer feels when he visits. We want them to feel comfortable, but they do not need to meet everybody. They are on a need-to-know basis. The people they need to know are anyone who cannot give them a dime and anyone that is required to close the deal. Period. Nobody else.

PART IV
Money (The Second Half of the Deal)

○ ○

"They used to say that knowledge is power. I used to think so, but I now know that they mean money."

—Lord Byron

Congratulations. You've got them seated in your office. This is a milestone. It's the seventh inning of the game and time to stretch out. The game is not over. It has just become interesting. You have all the information you need and the time has come to use it. The difference between the top producer and the guy they let go is in how the information is used.

Turning Over the Customer

For those of you that work in a strict turnover (T.O.) dealership, now it is time to spin the customer to your closer. How you handle this should be directed by the man who is about to get the customer dropped in his lap. It is not up to me to decide how the turn should take place in your store. There are as many schools of thought on this topic as there are experienced closers taking turns.

The turn is a necessary tool. Like any tool, if used at the correct time for the correct reasons it will increase any chance of furthering the deal. That's what the turn is for; getting to the next step. It suggests that another person entering the deal is considerably better qualified to handle the situation being addressed. Whether it is answering questions regarding vehicle model and equipment selection on the lot or explaining purchase options in the box, the result should be the same. We should answer the customers' concerns and progress the deal to its natural end, the close.

Some salespeople wait until they have exhausted any chance of furthering the deal (as well as exhausted the customer). They burn the customer. The customer becomes emotionally and physically drained to a point that all they care about is leaving. They want to get away from any interaction and rest their head. They have been taxed to a point where they actually feel that they must go and do not have any congenial blood running through their veins. The person that normally would not say anything that may be construed as rude may be so out of sorts that he actually insults you and walks away. The customer is burnt because the only way that we'll see him again is with another salesperson or in service with the vehicle he bought elsewhere.

When I first started in the business I asked my father how I would know when to turn a customer. He replied that my intuition will guide me on the lot and the desk manager will guide me in the box. He added that he turns every person who does not laugh at his jokes. This makes sense due to the fact that a customer is either comfortable and laughs due to humor or laughs to make a person feel good. If the customer does not care about you in the slightest then they most likely will not laugh even to appease you. If they will not smile when you say something that seems intended as a positive attempt to entertain them, then they probably wont spend thirty or forty thousand dollars with you until they bleed you of every possible cent that they can get. Life is too short to deal with these kinds of people. Turn them.

If you are going to turn customers in the box I suggest that you do so while they are seated with some sort of task. I use the phone, asking them to answer it if it were to ring. They watch the phone and not the time while I leave to retrieve the closer who I feel would best shut the deal or whomever the desk manager decides to turn the deal to if I don't have any input in the matter. Remember, while you are away from the customer time drags for them. Return as quickly as possible.

Never mention that you are going to get the manager up front. If you do many customers become apprehensive. They may not honestly wish to take the manager's time, afraid that doing so may obligate them (if only within their minds alone). If you state that you want to show them something and tell them to "wait here," they will. They wonder what it is you have that is so important for them to see. They'll wait a few minutes to satisfy their curiosity.

Your closer should already know that you have someone waiting for him. If he has done his job he has been watching you off and on throughout the steps of the sale and has timed the rest of his sales team so he can be prepared for the introduction you are about to give him.

As well, you should know when he is with another customer or assisting another salesperson. When necessary, you can bend time here and there with conversation that is proactive to the deal. If you do not know what to say to the customer then say nothing. Instead ask something about them. Remember, they love talking about themselves. Let them.

Every closer differs with what information they want you to provide them prior to turning. Some want a complete write-up. Others may want nothing at all on paper. I ask for a quick story, where the customer is from and what brought them to the dealership. From these items I can put my deal together as well as feel confident that the salesperson queried enough to suggest that they have built some rapport throughout their interactions with the customer.

The actual turn itself is a transfer of trust. The customer has built this trust in you and prefers not to be without you. You have become his security blanket. He feels that you will do the best job for him since you know so much about him and his motivations for purchasing, as well as whatever personal commonalities you share.

If you start early in the deal, planting a very small seed here and there about the closer who you know will be seeing the customer later, your turn will come easier for them. My favorite salesperson is a man named Ovie.

His turns were set up exactly as described. He'd chuckle at some point during the presentation of the vehicle. He'd often go on until the customer bought in. When the customer asked what he was laughing at he'd say something like, "I'm sorry. My wife and I took our granddaughter over to Tony, my manager's house for a family get together last week. You know how funny children can be at times. He has three boys. They were playing cowboys and Indians with Sarah, my granddaughter, in his backyard. They were running around whooping and hollering when one of them stopped suddenly and screamed for the others to do so as well. We were all caught off guard and so I asked across the yard, 'What's wrong?' He looked at me with this bewildered expression and asked, 'Uncle Ovie, why do they call them cowboys when they all ride horses?'"

This sort of set-up makes an indelible impression upon the customer. It has nothing to do with anything that they are there for. Yet it plants many seeds, comforts the customer, and makes it very difficult for the customer to forget that we are all like him. We are just normal people.

When you turn the customer to your closer, do so while you are sitting down with the customer. "Mr. and Mrs. Customer, this is Tony, my manager. He's the guy I told you about whose kid asked why they call themselves cowboys. Tony, This is Mr. and Mrs. Customer. Can you help us find a way to put this car in their driveway today?"

Your eye contact should be with the person you are addressing. First the customer and then the closer. After you finish making your statement, stand up and let the closer sit down. You are showing your respect for his position and that respect is evident in you giving up your seat for him.

Whenever the customer asks a question, smile and look at the customer while he asks it. Then turn to your closer and wait for him to answer. Even if the question is posed to you, the answer should come from the closer. If the closer wants you to speak he will ask for your input. Keep it brief while you answer the closer.

It makes sense to answer in a questioning manner, as if looking for the closer's agreement on whatever answer you give. For instance, if the customer asked you how much the stereo you shared with him would cost in his monthly payment, the closer would not have any idea which stereo the customer was referring to. Instead the closer would look at you and say, "Which stereo did you share with him?" You would look at the closer and answer, "I showed them the premium stereo. Wasn't it around $895? What would that do to their payment?" Let the closer answer.

Your eyes are on the closer and not the customer. This keeps the attention and focus on the person who is shutting the deal. It requires everyone to direct their attention to the closer. Your attention to what is being shared by the closer dictates where the customer will place his attention.

When the closer leaves the box do not follow him. Stay in the box with the customer and talk about the weather, places to eat, things you have in common, etc. Any reference to the deal or monies now must be handled with a statement that encourages both you and the customer to address the closer when he returns. Make it something like, "Good question. Remind we to ask him when he gets back. So how about them Raiders, eh?"

If the concern is important to the customer then they will need to bring it up. You suddenly forgot about it. You had asked them to remind you, remember? They cannot be upset with you. It's their fault they didn't remind you.

Occasionally the customer will ask for a few minutes to think about the deal or discuss it privately. You want to keep them seated. However, you are not in control of the customer or deal any longer. Refer to the closer. He will tell them to go ahead and chat while you both leave. Do not go off into another room or out of sight from the customer if you can avoid it. I prefer to stand just outside the office, beyond perceived earshot, and let the closer go wherever he wants. If you follow him the customer thinks you're conspiring against him. Do not give him any reason to feel this way.

Step #7: The Write-Up

There are some basics that we should discuss regarding your office. I am amazed that I need to bring them up to begin with at times. My salespeople are smart guys yet there is always that yahoo whom the world revolves around. He's that guy who doesn't think and walks in on you and your deal right when you are waiting on your close. He helps the customer say "no."

It's like I'm fishing. I spent all my dough on a nice rod and reel. My tackle box is chocked with every lure that money can buy. I have come prepared. I cast my line at just the right distance into the right spot. The fish is there. That big guy that nobody has caught for years. The fish that stories are told of every night for generations. He's about to take my line and... "*BLAM!*"...some idiot decides to take a dive in the water and interrupt my groove.

What do you have in your office? Is it only your stuff or are you sharing either the office or the equipment with another salesperson? There is no reason for anyone ever to walk in and disturb you when you are "in the box." If someone died, you probably are not going to change the fact that they are dead. If they didn't die yet then, unless you're a doctor, you still aren't going to help much. Especially if you don't have enough money for the co-pay for the emergency room because someone screwed up your closing ratio while letting you know about this horrible news.

You do not walk in on someone else and they do not walk in on you. I believe that a simple rule could remedy this problem if well applied: "If you walk in on someone in the box, you're fired. End of story."

Another pet peeve of mine is when a salesperson answers the phone while a customer is in the box with him or has gone to the bathroom. The phone is not there for you to talk on while you're busy with a breathing customer.

Think of it this way. The phone is to bring people in to the store so you can carve them. If you already have someone in front of you then you have a great chance at making a deal. The customer could say, "Okay, let's do this," at any given moment. You need to be there, pushing every button, smiling and getting the customer to answer your questions until his head is spinning and he says, "Okay." You need to be ready to tell them how much to write the check for at all times. Answer the phone when they're in finance, or better yet, wait until they drive off in their new car.

Do not let them stand up for any reason. If they need to use the restroom then you've been in the close too long or they've had too much to drink. Standing up means they're stretching their legs. Let them stretch their legs on their way to their new car. They can go to the park or their friend's house after they sign up. They don't need to go hiking around your dealership. Your dealership doesn't have nature trails running around it for a reason.

Every time you stand up they may want to do the same. Keep them seated by asking them to answer the phone when it rings. You happen to be waiting for an important call from your wife, lover, girlfriend, boyfriend, mother, whatever. This does two things. It makes you sound human. You have a family or people you love who love you. It also gives them a task when you leave so that they don't start walking around, staring at their watch. Make them feel important to you and they'll make you proud.

Body Language

Have you ever had a person you know run into you on the street or at a party when you were preoccupied? Perhaps you didn't want to get involved in a lengthy conversation. You didn't want to be mean and you didn't want to hurt their feelings, but your lack of desire for any conversation with this person outweighs these other concerns. You are uncomfortable. You force poor eye contact, look at your watch a couple times within a single minute, and maybe even gesture that you have to leave. It doesn't faze them. They go on without any cognitive response to your needs.

For them it's as if you are family they haven't seen in years. You see them as the neighbor of a friend whom the friend has never liked.

Do not be like this person. Be aware of what the other person is saying with his body. Watch their movements. Do they reach for their purse? Adust their clothes? Sit forward in their chair? Look over their shoulder? Could you make some irrelevant statement about the size of their nose and only get an "oh" or "uh-huh" from them?

By insisting that you be aware, I am not saying that you should allow them to leave when they begin exhibiting some form of uneasy, non-verbal gesture. It isn't time to cut them loose. It's time to start paying attention to what you're doing.

What is your body language feeding them? Is your appearance a problem? Are you sitting too close, with horrible breath? If you're a smoker, have you washed your hands or brushed your teeth lately? Are you one of those people who are constantly covered in sweat? Change what you have control over. What you cannot change, find a better way to mask.

If you are doing or saying something that tends to drop your customers' attention at a specific point in every deal, then you should take note. Remember when and where it is happening. What are the circumstances? Perhaps, just prior to the next time you sense that you will find yourself at this perilous stage of the deal, you should immediately turn the customer to another salesperson. Half of something is better than all of nothing.

I often do this myself. If the customer isn't laughing at my jokes I turn them. Not because I feel I'm a funny person whom everyone must laugh at. I know that I'm not that funny. It's because I know my jokes are corny and a person whom I have control over will give at least one mercy giggle if he feels the least bit of empathy for someone as obviously dim as I am. I turn them immediately and I walk away.

<u>Information</u>

I have tossed around whether or not to include much information in the write-up section of this book. Knowing that potential customers may read it has weighed heavily on my decision to leave my personal write-up out. It is not my write-up that matters anyway. Sure, I'd like to say that you will do well by writing everybody the exact way that I do. Unfortunately, I cannot in good conscience make that statement.

There are two factors that influence whether a deal is going to close or not: the information I am getting from the customer and how this information is used. Since I do not know what each customer is going to share with you, I cannot guide you on what to say. That is the duty of your desk manager. He needs to be a part of your negotiations.

Sure, there are many trainers who can toss random phrases out that may help you in specific closing situations. I enjoy using canned statements to get specific responses. It is necessary to have an artillery of choice words ready for any objection. I am not here to give them to you. You will find a few within these pages, but my duty as I see it is to encourage you to experience the deal from a freely behavioral position.

Train with other trainers as often as possible to gather one-liners that might help you when you have nothing else to say that is unique. Train with your co-workers daily when you need a fresh look at handling an objection that a customer gave you a difficult time with. Usually directly after a customer leaves the dealership (or your company) is a good time to ask others what they would have done or how they would have answered. Buy books. Listen to tapes. Watch other salespeople work. Be a sponge.

More importantly, ask your desk manager for guidance as to how he would handle that situation. You truly are an extension of him. You will be talking to the customer for him. That is your job as well as his. He didn't get where he's at because he's the owner's kid. Even owners don't promote their children if they're idiots. They promote the guy who will close the most deals for the most money. Trust these guys.

<u>Numbers Game</u>

Remember, this is a numbers game. The more you meet, the more you drive, the more you write, the more you close. If you put every hand you shake on paper you will lead the board in sales. Simple fact.

I waste more paper than anybody I know. When a customer asks anything about a figure I write him up. If they were to ask if the bathroom had one or two stalls I'd write them. If they asked how many children I had or what my favorite number is they'd find themselves in a box with me scribbling on a worksheet, telling stories and relating optional financing for them to take home their new car.

I write everything that I say and nothing that they say. Some people are visual while others need auditory input. It doesn't matter for me. I allow them to understand what I am saying via either form of absorption, but only when I am sharing my numbers with them.

If I write any numbers that the customer may have in mind then I am only putting weight on their figures. I'm substantiating the value that they have placed in these numbers. I'm "listening" and "understanding" the customer, and this creates a poor space for me to work my way out of. Their numbers are like the air they were breathed into: gone. There is no proof that they were ever mumbled. It's only the customer's word against yours. Why cloud things up by having to prove that?

Use Your Store's Program

Remember that a close is a natural end to a good presentation, and a close with gross is a natural end to a great presentation. If you have completed the steps at a comfortable pace and established proper control of your customer then the write-up is merely a formality. The customer should be handing you his checkbook and asking you to go ahead and fill in the amount for him to sign. Anything other than that and you are negotiating.

Every dealership has its own way of writing a customer. Sometimes within a dealership there may be more than one way to complete a write-up that is acceptable by the desk manager. Whatever the situation, you must be aware that the desk manager leads the deal. He is the director and you are the actor. He will tell you what to do and say as well as train you on how he wants to begin the negotiations that he orchestrates. Take his lead. Allow him to train you. It is within this training, and the training of whomever replaces him, and whom he replaced, that you will learn where your talents within the write-up flourish.

This is where the dust settles. The seeds you have planted throughout your deal are ready to be harvested. Your memory (and lack of memory, when appropriate) are crucial to your closing success. Couple this, the immediate attention of a good desk manager, with your ability to take direction from him and you will close the deals that nobody else could.

First Numbers & Influence

One of the reasons you do not want to write everything your customer says has to do with affirming the "credibility" of his offer. We never want them to feel that they are offering something that is acceptable or possible upon first pencil. If we do give them any form of affirmation, we are handing them control of the deal. They now have the green light to walk out on us no matter if we accept their offer or not.

I prefer to influence all of my customers' offers prior to them becoming known. As a salesperson I would give the customer monthly figures loosely based on basic math for forty-eight months at around 12 percent APR. I never told the customer that this was the calculation. I merely stated that the payment would be "X" and waited to see where they landed.

This is why money is only talked while the customer is sitting down inside the box. If for some reason the customer is launched when the numbers come out, he will not go into orbit and be able to leave the atmosphere or dealership too easily.

Instead, his head will stick in the sheet rock and we can pull him out by his ankles.

If the customer does not ask a question as to the term or the interest rate then so be it. There is no reason to discuss elements of the deal that are not a concern to the customer. Wait and listen to your customers and they will tell you where they want to be. They will give you a straight verbal answer that has now been influenced by your larger-than-life first number or they will grab their purse and adjust their belt to leave. Either way you have helped them in starting the negotiation. Now you ask, "Right where you want to be, right?"

Some salespeople feel that they do not want to be the "bad guy" or play like they are stupid. They do not want to give numbers that are not straightforward and accurate. I understand these wants.

I would prefer to be straightforward as well. However, when I have done so the customer always asks for less. They almost never just say "okay." Those that did almost always couldn't finance the sesame seeds on a hamburger bun. Or they stood to leave after saying that everything was perfect and when they "are ready to buy, they'll be back," because they "like me so much." All crap. They're never coming back if I let them leave.

Why would I want to waste a customer's precious time by letting him leave the dealership and have to schedule to come back and start over with his purchase? It is a disservice to the customers to poorly influence them and keep them from driving home in a new car.

Some salespeople feel that they should get their first numbers from the desk manager. The problems with doing this are numerous. It allows your customer an extra few minutes in the box waiting for you to return, wondering why it is taking you so long. They are already wondering why they are sitting there since they had told you that they were "just shopping" and now they are asking themselves why you didn't hear them.

The figures they see first are coming from "God," with his all-knowing calculator, and therefore the accuracy alone which you are suggesting by presenting numbers this way is not conducive to beginning any negotiations. Think of it this way. If you had to leave to get the numbers, you obviously aren't very successful. You don't know the math relevant to your job. Why should they buy from you? If you returned without any sort of discount for them which they perceive as "working for them," then why should they give you their money? On the other hand, why should the dealership employ you if you are going to give money away before the negotiations begin?

When you work out the figure in front of them, not only do you give the illusion of credibility, but you also put weight in the human element. If they are smart enough to do some basic math they may ask you what you're doing and begin to tell you how crazy you are. You have influenced them still and they will make an offer and commitment in one breath. You can simply act like you must have made a mistake and then accept the fact that your math abilities are poor. This gives you a reason to go to the desk, as well as gives them a reason to tell you what they were hoping to achieve. The negotiations begin.

Now the desk can come back with figures as well as direction that will progress the deal to its natural end: the close.

What is a Commitment?

Have you heard or used "if I could…would you…" or "what is it going to take…"? It happens to me everywhere I've worked and to every salesperson I have known. It happens to me. We've all done it. We're lazy. We want the deal quickly and we're ready to "Make it happen."

Unfortunately this is not possible. We do not eat an elephant in one bite. It takes hundreds of little bites. We need to take our time and chew our food well. The close comes within the time we are taking as we get to know the customer. The continued stomping of their hot buttons, which we have discovered during this bite-by-bite routine, adds weight.

Besides, if the customer were to tell us that he would buy the vehicle today if we were to complete a number of specific tasks, both monetary and physical, we would find that the customer may be lying. We call this a commitment. It's not. It's an opportunity for us to confront customers if they back out of their agreement with us after we've worked to get it approved. It's a quick way through to the end of the deal, even if the end comes with the customer not driving home in our car. It's a short cut. We end up with bruised knees and they leave in the car they arrived in. It's a negotiation, not a confrontation. Why put ourselves into a position that doesn't benefit us?

The only real commitment I know of comes when I see brake lights going over the curb. Those customers are committed. Nobody else.

Trade In

It was a Saturday morning. Myself and a co-worker both had early bird deals while trying to grab at some spiff money before lunch. As luck would have it we both had customers' cars we needed to get appraised. The used car manager's office was down the street at the other showroom. In a hurry to get our respective customers into the finance office first, we raced down the street in these trade ins. I was leading most of the way until he swerved in front of me while I slowed for the entrance to the parking lot. Hitting the curb sideways, his car tipped and rolled onto its roof. The car spun, sliding about a hundred yards or so until it came to rest just outside the used car manager's office. The manager walked out as the vehicle stopped in front of him. Without blinking, the manager took the appraisal slip from the salesperson, who was a bit out of breath and hanging from his seatbelt, still fastened, retraining him in his seat. The manager wrote $200 on the slip and stated to the sales person: "I would've given you $800 had it been on its wheels."

When those of us who have been in the automotive business for any period of time are prepared, nothing seems to faze us. We are a deadly bunch to play poker with. Our faces are used to telling stories and our intuition is programmed to know a lie. We are unbeatable when we know what is coming next. It is the uncertainty of any situation that has the potential to throw us from our game.

It is interesting that we become so bothered when the customer tosses in a trade in after the deal is negotiated. We know that every "How to Buy a Car" book exploits this ploy. However, we are armed with enough information to stop this sort of behavior.

Is it that we feel slighted by the fact that this ploy is rather ridiculous to begin with? Are we only upset with ourselves for not asking for the trade in in other ways or not finding out how this person typically deals with his old cars? Perhaps there is something in us all that expects the customer to have a small amount of respect for us, enough to be willing to show how important the trade is to him early on in the deal.

Whatever the case we need to explore how we ask for the trade. Whenever we are not getting the answers we need when we need them, we should take a closer look at what we are asking as well as how we are asking. I prefer to be straightforward with the customer during both the "determining needs" as well as the "write up" steps to the sale.

Questions like "Who are you giving your old car to, a neighbor or a relative?" will provide answers and insight that may surprise you. They will fill your head with information that you can use later in the close. Try a question like, "How do they like your last car?" implying the vehicle that was "given" to their family or friend in the past. Similar responses as before will be insightful. Customers' non-verbal reactions often inform you of their emotional tie to the vehicle.

As always, first you learn what the customer's input is. You collect the information. Then you understand how the information can be used. Later, when it is important to do so, you exploit it.

When putting the customer on paper I enjoy asking if I can "show the deal both ways?" When the customer inquires as to what I mean by both ways or just says "yes" I answer, "Good, we'll see it with and without the trade." I offer no eye contact when I begin my pencil and the customer will almost always pipe up with vigor as to whether they intend to trade or not. I do not intend to actually show the deal any other way then the way they wish to continue, unless the need arises to manipulate the figures in my favor one way or the other.

Like I stated before, I prefer to influence the customer every time money is involved. When it comes to giving the customer figures on their trade I prefer to begin influencing them early in the deal.

For an example, let me share how I handle a typical lunch buyer with you. The person comes in around noon, dressed as if they are working in whatever your area's demographics may be. Whether they are wearing a workplace uniform or business suit, they are most certainly walking with conviction and looking at the time. They move from their car quickly since they have little time to waste and they may even come directly into the showroom to "pick up some quick information." They are direct and to the point. "Got a brochure? How much is this? How much is that? What's my trade worth?"

I encourage you to stand as far away from the customer's vehicle as possible when you try this out. Ask them, while peering from across the street, if they purchased paint and fabric protection when they purchased that car. Whether they ask why you need to know or not doesn't matter. You then add the benefit: "If you did, then the vehicle would be worth more upon trade in. The reconditioning would be less. We have even had vehicles repainted entirely under warranty of the contracting company when they lost their shine. We pass that savings along to you."

This type of discussion shows that you are working for an intelligent dealership who knows how to save money and please a customer. It also influences the customer by decreasing the value they will accept for their trade without you ever giving them a figure. No matter what they were thinking, now they'll accept less.

Do not give this person a number on their trade, as you will never see them again unless you give away all the money. We do not want to do that yet we need to see them again. Set an appointment when you intend to get back to them within the day. Find the best way to reach them while they are at work. Go to their business and drop off the vehicle they were inquiring about. Pick up their trade and bring it back to the dealership for the specialist that you have "dropping by later in the day" to evaluate. They'll come in, driving their new car, after they get out, and you can give your used car manager a lengthy opportunity to find the gold bars hidden in the trunk of their car. Everybody wins. They've returned and you have them.

You're not going to sell them over the phone. Do not call them. Go see them. Take something they have. They'll come get it if you are offering something they want. Especially if you have their car. Try it.

Step #8: Finance & Insurance

Many salespeople want only to close the deal. That's all they are concerned with. They feel that they ostensibly have their money and they have pulled the customer to a point of uncomfortableness so they do not want to bring up anything that may jeopardize their deal. Sometimes they actually kick opportunities in an effort to close the deal to begin with. As long as they made their money they are fine.

Rocky was the name of my favorite F&I manager. I believed he was like a god. I'd take the customer for a couple hundred dollars more than they wanted to spend per month, stretching them out to "not a penny more than" and drop them in his office. However, always prior to bringing the customer in I'd lean over his desk and say, "Please be careful. I got these people to buy today. They were just shopping and somehow they're okay spending a few bucks more for the car, but please don't mention a service contract or alarm. They'll bolt. I'm telling ya, don't do it. I need the deal" or something like that, with a little more begging.

Rocky was great. He'd listen to my entire song and dance with compassion in his voice and agree to "breeze through the contract." He didn't want the store to lose the deal on account of his greed. What a team player he was.

Well, just as often as I prepared Rocky for my cheapskate customers he managed to bump them another fifty dollars a month or get another three grand from them for some back end item he sold. I couldn't understand it. How was he doing it? Wasn't he listening to me? Obviously not. *He didn't know that he couldn't do it.* I was unclear when trying to communicate this fact to him. He was good to not rub my face in it.

One day he approached me to congratulate me on another plaque for "Salesman of the Month." I had beaten the next guy by seven cars. He asked how much money I had made in doing this. When I answered him he showed me the other guy's paycheck. To my astonishment it was a few hundred dollars more than mine. A bit taken back, I questioned how this could be possible. He said, "You get paid on back end money."

All this time I had been shooting myself in the foot by not setting up his opportunities. Instead I encouraged many of his failures by doing the opposite with the customers before introducing them to him.

Rocky was someone that I looked up to. His words were few and those he chose to share were appropriate. He pointed out to me that if I spent the same amount of time with the customer preparing them for his options that I usually spent preparing him, he would have greater success. His success would be my windfall. No time would go wasted on energy working against the deal.

I am grateful to Rocky for the fact that my paycheck doubled during many months of mediocre sales. This chapter explains how we made that happen, together.

Improving the Deal

The farmer does not drop seeds from his pocket and pull fruit from the ground during the same moment. It takes weeks and often months for his labors to produce a product. How can we expect anything different?

Within the "Meet and Greet" we can begin planting our seeds. Asking whether a customer purchased a service contract on his last vehicle during this stage will offer us an opportunity to understand the customer and his buying habits. If they question us on why we want to know this information or are reluctant to give us an answer that we feel is truthful, we must have a reason why we have asked this question. The reason is the benefit.

Always offer a benefit for any product that you are planting a seed for. The benefit to a service contract could be expressed in many ways. I usually state, "The reason I asked is so when I take your trade to the used car manager I can tell him that any concerns were repaired under warranty with genuine factory parts. This adds value to your trade and if it is still in effect, could keep the costs of reconditioning down. Again, more money for you."

The customer understands this type of talk. More money is what they want to hear. Whether or not they have a trade or they purchase service contracts is what you want to know. Carry this information with you throughout the deal.

During the write-up you will once again mention the service contract simply by adding the cost of it in to the price of the vehicle before giving the customer any figures whatsoever. You do not have to quote an exact contract with terms and deductibles. Use a standard contract that the majority of your customers in that specific demographic buy. Use a list price that is acceptable from your desk manager. Figure it in payments with any other options that you have done the same thing with and then present them to the customer.

If the customer balks at anything included in your figures, you now have something to take away without affecting your price and front end gross profit. "The payment will be a few bucks less then, Mr. Customer." If the items have become a must-have for your customer, then you know that you have more hot buttons to work with to make a deal.

Service Contracts

I prefer to sell only factory service contracts. Many stores sell aftermarket contracts that may leave the customer waiting for approval from a third party insurer prior to having service work performed. The waiting could and usually does cause grief; lost work time, no rental car, missed personal appointments and functions…the list goes on. This weakens your chances of ever selling, let alone seeing, that customer for his next purchase.

Some customers buy their own third party service contract. They are being offered by credit unions, insurance companies, and even online vendors for next-to-nothing prices. Customers that buy these are typically unhappy when they need them. I've seen fistfights over what the customer feels should be covered and what control the dealership has with these contracts. Unfortunately, it is always the dealership and you who loses when these contracts do not perform. Seems that the money the customer saved only cost you in the long run.

If possible, discourage this type of behavior without hurting your relationship with the customer. If it feels as if it may mar your ability to positively persuade the customer regarding other portions of the deal then drop it. Do not reinforce their buying decision for the third party contract. You will become the heal twice if you do.

Mention that factory service contracts are often refundable. Many manufacturers pro-rate a refund for the unused portion of the service contract if a customer sells or trades their car prior to the miles or date that the contract was good through.

Another nice facet of the factory service contract deals with transferability. Perhaps the customer has a romantic idea that he will sell his car himself. The contract could go with the car, increasing the value of a used car drastically. Private party buyers place great value on vehicles which have factory warranty or service contracts still in effect.

I must mention that I do not buy a car without purchasing a service contract myself. My family cannot buy from me without doing the same. I refuse to stand in the service department listening to people I care about ask how they will be getting to work.

Paint & Fabric Protection

This profit making option has a very bad reputation, which we have created. Through derogatory nick names, dealerships not applying it at all, and F&I managers overcharging for these options all together, we have minimized our ability to sell it. The item itself is a fantastic benefit to the customer if the customer is one of those people who likes to detail his car every six months. It aids in keeping the vehicle looking new.

Find out how your store handles the process, who applies it, and what kind of job they do. The experience of having the product applied should be seamless for the customer. Many times this is the customer's first experience with any "service" work completed on his car. Even if your service department doesn't apply the product, the customer believes that it did. Your dealership's relationship with the customer is based on this experience.

If the experience is going to be a poor one and the task to get the item applied is cumbersome then you should discuss this with your immediate manager. Ask for his guidance on the issue. Ask him what he would like you to do about it for your share of the sale.

I plant my seeds for this product in the same manner as I do for the service contract. It begins in the "Determining Needs" portion of the deal. I ask if their trade had this product applied to it. If it had, "then the used car manager will need to know. It may make their trade worth more, since reconditioning the paint or fabric would cost us less. We pass this savings along to you, Mr. Customer..."

This allows me once again to understand what type of customer I am dealing with as well as prepare them for the opportunity to increase their vehicle's value for a future trade. It also gives me a reason to go ask for more money, if needed, when I hit them low for their trade on first pencil. "The used car manager must not know that your trade has paint and fabric protection. Let me chat with him about your trade's value." It keeps the customers seated while you go looking for more money for them. When you return with a "few bucks more," it helps close your current deal as well as build value via paint and fabric protection for their new vehicle.

Alarms & Radios

Anything that takes the integrity of the vehicle's electrical system into account is another factory only sale for me. I need to know that if something breaks on the customer's car it will be fixed. The phone call from an irate customer who is locked out of his new car on his first vacation trip across the country while I try to make a living is something I'd prefer to go without.

The phone call from a customer who finds the radio I just installed for him in a newspaper advertisement for three hundred dollars less than I sold it to him for is also not a necessity for me on a busy day. You may say, "Then don't sell it for so much." I apologize. I have to.

Think of it this way: If I get twenty percent of the profit and I sell an item for which the customer has to take time out of his busy day to come visit me, I will undoubtedly be missing something on my end. Either I will not be training, helping another customer buy a car, or teaching my kids to throw a baseball. Something will have to give so that I may be waiting for this customer in the service department when he shows up.

What is my time worth? The car is already sold. Why possibly destroy the customer's relationship with the dealership over twenty bucks? How about a hundred? In order to do that I must sell a two-hundred dollar stereo for twelve hundred dollars. How will I look now?

Paperwork

Every store is different when it comes to how much and what type of paperwork you will handle. Whatever your role dictates that you complete, I encourage you to complete it thoroughly unless directed otherwise by your management staff. Why do the same job more than once?

I use the paperwork as a means to recall as much about the customer as I can. Reviewing some common ground and past history information that they have given me exhibits the fact that I listened to them and builds credibility. It also allows for them to feel increasingly comfortable with me. They're relaxing.

You can tell that they're comfortable when they have their purse or wallet opened up and spread all over your desk. Maybe they're sitting back in their seat, allowing you to roam around in their stuff. (Don't go as far as to do that. Something might turn up missing. We all know who stole whatever turns up missing, right? That "salesman." Be aware of how comfortable they are, however.)

When they're comfortable and the paperwork is complete you will be taking your last swing at improving the deal prior to leaving them with the F & I manager.

Introducing the F & I Manager

Without getting into stereotypes again, let me just ask you what you've heard about the F&I manager. What stories do you have or have you heard about the type of shenanigans that go on in that office? It's a bad place. Has a bad sound. Carries a bad rap. Don't take your customer there.

Let's change the name. Make it something comfortable that the customer is not expecting. Even if they read the book on "How to Buy a Car," they will not know immediately that the person you are turning them to happens to be the same guy that they were warned about. Perhaps they will never know until it is too late. They went and spoke to this guy and now they have formed positive opinions about him. They like him. They cannot un-like him because of the book they read or prejudices they were predisposed to. They're going to have to go on liking him and make up their own excuses for doing so later.

For now on we'll call the F & I manager the Business Manager. He will handle all of the business paperwork and registration portion of the deal. He's the guy who dots the i's and crosses the t's. As a courtesy, he gets the financing handled for the customers so that they can avoid wasting any of their valuable time dragging their transportation needs out any longer than necessary.

The way I introduce the customer begins with reaffirming the after-market options I want them to buy. My monologue goes like this:

"In a moment I'm going to take you to complete the registration portion of the deal. I'll be getting your new vehicle ready, gassing it up and cleaning it. So you know, we are not like the other dealerships who try to shove a bunch of stuff into the deal which wouldn't help you."

I wait for them to sigh or say "good" or any other response they wish to mutter. Then I continue, "I have handpicked a few items that, if you were my family, I'd encourage you to purchase. First, the factory service contract. It's a must. It's not like those after-market contracts that many dealerships sell. The ones that do not transfer or cover anything that breaks. They're a bit more in price but well worth it."

I try to go ahead without pausing but sometimes I'm stopped with questions about coverage. This is okay. It's a wonderful opportunity to segue into the introduction: "In a moment I'll introduce you to the business manager who can answer those exact questions for you. So you know, one way we keep the costs of our service contracts down here at this dealership is we keep from allowing a bunch of salespeople to sell them. Without all the salespeople earning commission, we can afford to sell them at these ridiculous prices." This usually stops the customers, and they allow you to continue. If they do not then just say, "No problem," and go on.

"Second, as we discussed earlier regarding your trade's value, the paint and fabric protection will add hundreds to your vehicle's value upon trade in with me here at this dealership when you're ready. Please listen to the benefits so you can make an intelligent decision to buy."

If they ask how much it is you can relate back to their trade in and hit them with a few hundred over retail. In my store retail was $499. I told them, "It is typically sold for $799 in most stores, yet once again, since we keep the salespeople out of the equation the business manager will offer it for less. We'll ask him what it is.

"Finally, alarms. You mentioned how you are concerned with someone stealing your new car. You really need to protect your investment."

My spiel was usually about four minutes. The business manager let me know when he was ready for the customer. He knew I'd be with them for four minutes and then he'd page me to bring them to him or he'd come and get them. Our timing was designed to make sure that they were put in his hands when they started asking questions. Four minutes was just about right for me every time. You'll have to try it find your own time, but I encourage you to keep it close to the same four minutes. Anything longer and the customer begins to get anxious. Anything shorter and the perceived value of what you are sharing is lost. If you aren't going to spend time on it then it must not be worth much.

When I introduced the customer to the business manager I would make eye contact with the customer and say, "Mr Customer, this is Mr. Smith, the business manager I told you about. He's amazing. He's been with the dealership" (or in the business, whichever is the most impressive) "for 'X' years. His talent is truly an asset to the dealership." Then I would shift eye contact, looking only at the business manager. "Mr. Smith, Mr. Customer and I have discussed a few options that we believe would benefit him. He would like to hear about the service contract because" (insert whatever reason is relevant to the customer; you should have one by now). "Also, the paint and fabric protection would be good for reselling his vehicle in the future. Please discuss it as well as an alarm system since" (whatever reason, once again, you have collected).

Turn back to the customer and thank him with proper eye contact. Let him know that you'll be back shortly as well as the fact that he is "with the best guy in the dealership." Thank the business manager using "Mr. Smith, thank you" and walk away.

You have just transferred your trust in the business manager to the customer. He will now sit back a little easier and listen to what is being said since you've encouraged him to do so. Now the business manager does not have to bring up these items as if they're separate from the deal. They seem like items that must be discussed for your benefit as well as the customer's. They will be reviewed and most likely purchased.

Step #9: Get the Vehicle Ready

Who is responsible for preparing the vehicle in your dealership? In almost every case it is you. Sure you may have porters that work with you, but remember that they are hourly employees. They do not get surveys on how they performed. Their paycheck is not reflective of how many cars they've washed for you.

If it is late at night they will probably have left already. They left when the clock rang, or hid from you until it did, then left. They're gone and who has to take care of the car? You do.

There have been many nights where we closed a deal at midnight and the porter had long since left. I rolled up my sleeves and went outside to wash a car. I don't have a problem getting dirty. I am the General Sales Manager and I believe in never asking my guys to do something that I wouldn't do myself.

I will say that whenever I did wash a customer's car, I asked the salesperson to pull his customers out of the business office when he was done making this statement: "Hey, Mr. and Mrs. Customer. You have got to see this. Our porters are gone. The big boss wants everything to be perfect for you so he is out here right now. Come see this." Saying these words with laughter and excitement, mixed with the deliriousness of a midnight deal, makes the customer feel special. They walk out and see me covered in suds or drying their car. "This is Mr. Ziegler. He's the General Sales Manager."

"Thanks for your business folks. Sorry it's so late. Have you out of here in a jiffy" is my regular response. The customer's response is always "100 percent" on the survey they get.

If your manager will not get dirty do not fear. You will get dirty for him. He can turn the tables and bring your customer out to you washing the car. The result is the same: A very satisfied customer.

Some salespeople ask the customer to return to get their car "detailed." They think they're doing them a favor. Instead they are allowing the customer to find problems with the car which they will need to address when the customer does bring the car in. When they arrive, they will undoubtedly be taking the salesperson away from another potential sale. If they allow the salesperson to continue to work while they wait for their car to be cleaned, then they'll feel slighted in some manner. They'll walk around and hear other salespeople closing deals or see advertisement figures or color choices they hadn't noticed before. Something will become an issue. Your survey score will suffer.

Get them done once. Get them gone. Bring them back when you want them to return. Keep them away from the dealership until it benefits you.

Detail vs. Cleanup

When you are referring to the cleanup of the customer's new car you should avoid using any words that sound as if there will be something special done to that car. You are giving them a service given to every customer because your store treats every customer special. You are washing their car. Nothing else. If you use the word "detail," then you will undoubtedly see the customer again and again while every scratch and nick is uncovered and examined.

Most stores charge the salesperson for spending money after the close of the sale. If the deal is done and items you have mentioned are not included in the negotiations, then you will be the one paying for them. Make sure all concerns are addressed within the close. They can easily be kicked when shaking hands and must always be fixed when not addressed properly.

Preparing the Drive Off

Once the vehicle is clean it should be pointing toward the curb. You want your customer to walk out of the business office and quickly review any warranty and owner's manual information in your office. When that is complete you need to be able to walk them directly to their new vehicle, where you can give them a once over before letting them leave.

I like to walk them through the vehicle in the same fashion that I had during the "Presentation" step. It should be quicker, since you know their hot buttons. You can push a few of them to help reinforce their buying decision. Program their radio for them while showing them how to do it themselves. Have them in the driver seat when you are finished and the drive off will be easy.

With the vehicle pointed at the curb there will be no problem with them backing their new car into the wall or another person's car. It happens. Don't let it happen to you.

Dennis was a salesperson who worked for my father. He hadn't sold a car in a week and the pressure was wearing him down. He was a good salesperson but the lack of a sale made him question and take short cuts.

Finally, on the last day of the month he managed to get the last deal out the door. It was a bonus car that made him a substantial amount of money. He didn't turn the car toward the open end of the lot, however. As his customer drove to the other end of the lot he stood yelling for them to stop. They were busy adjusting their seat and mirrors when they ran into a security chain, causing about two thousand dollars' damage. Since they hadn't actually left the lot yet the damage was on us.

To top it off they saw it as a sign that they shouldn't buy a car that night. They decided to sleep on it. They never returned. Dennis quit the next day. Now he sells timeshares in Georgia. They're already pointing in the wrong direction. There is nothing to run into that isn't already there.

Delivery Paperwork

Prior to the customer leaving the business office you should prepare your owner's manual and warranty books. Make sure that you know what is there to give to the customer. You don't need to start running around looking for tire warranty information with the customer waiting, so have it prepared and waiting for him.

Get the extra keys and whatever paperwork you will need to complete with them. If you are selling a new car there is typically more paperwork to get ready. New vehicle manufacturers have delivery check sheets of some form or another that focus on getting positive customer satisfaction scores. Be familiar with these forms and walk your customer through them quickly.

You've already sold the car. Don't waste your time dragging out a delivery that the customer is not listening to. They want to leave. They are salivating. Let them drive off and begin their new life.

If it is a used vehicle, then check the glove box for any paperwork that shouldn't be in the car. Past records and personal information of former owners is not beneficial for the new owner to find. Some of the information may queer your deal or contradict whatever you may have told them. You want the customer to have a fresh start.

People trade their trouble because they do not want to explain it to others. The last thing you want to do is allow your new customer to call someone who had nothing but problems with the car. If only for the problems, you want to keep them away from each other. Not to mention the money differences between what the store took the car in trade for and what it sold for. Sure, we all know that money had to be made somewhere. But try and explain to a customer that a four-thousand dollar difference is normal and you will be a liar as well as a thief.

Once the vehicle is facing in the right direction and the paperwork is ready you can bring the customer to your office. Review the printed information quickly by showing the customer how to find answers to whatever questions he will have in the future. Ask them if they understand and if they have any questions about what you shared.

Place your business card in their owner's manual and state that it is there for them to use whenever they have questions that they cannot find out the answers to on their own. If you do not do this you will field calls pertaining to stupid questions. Do you remember the person who once told you there are no stupid questions? That person was an idiot. Any question that one can determine the answer to oneself is a stupid question. It will not take long before your customer opens his owner's manual to look for your card to ask a question, but instead of calling you, he answers it himself. You're training them months after they leave. Good job.

Step #10: Delivery

Well they are ready. The paperwork is complete and their vehicle sits somewhere that is appealing and easy to drive away from. Your job is not over yet.

I do not have anybody else deliver my customers. I think it's wrong. After spending the last couple of hours wrapping this person up in our rapport and selling the fact that I will always be there for them, I do not want them to wonder where I went after they signed. No one will take the time that I will to reinforce the customer's buying decisions, of which only I am aware.

You have already done a good job of explaining much of the function of their new car during the presentation step of the deal. This is not a time to start talking about availability of options. Do not review what they could have bought. Review what they did buy that is relevant to the customers' expressed wants and needs. Keep it brief.

Try to already know what station the customer listens to on the radio. While you're sitting in their car beside them, show them how to program the radio using their favorite station. Wait while they program a couple themselves if they want to. Review the safety items: seat belts, mirrors, driver seat adjustment, tilt steering column, turn signals, emergency flashers, headlights, and windshield wipers.

Ask often whether there are any questions. They will not have many. If they do then listen and answer them concisely. Ask them, "Did I answer that well enough for you?" If you haven't they will speak up.

Once the customer seems ready to leave and he has no more questions, review your Sales Satisfaction Survey. Let the customer know that he will be receiving it and ask him to complete it and send it in. Tell him that it's your report card and you need the feedback to improve the way you do business.

The problem with surveys is getting satisfied customers to complete them. Sure, the guy who may have had a horrible experience for whatever reason will definitely send in a survey. You can guarantee that if you spit in the customer's face he will mention it. If you scratch your knees up for them you have a one in ten chance of being thanked.

I find it best to kick the survey with some suggestive influence if it is going to be bad. By letting the customer know that you "must have the survey returned as the fact alone of it being returned pays you dividends" that guy who doesn't like anybody to make money will not mail it. You can also state, "If you wish to destroy me then throw the thing in the trash." Pause shortly. Look the customer in the eye. Continue, "Do not do that! It will kill me." Consider that survey toast.

Some dealerships allow you to "burn" a survey here or there. So you know, it is not truly possible to do so with any regularity. The manufacturer wants to know what is going on at the dealership level. It's one of their ways of finding out. They do not allow this sort of picking and choosing who will be surveyed. Many are pretty strict about not burning surveys. I encourage you to use other ways to get rid of them.

Getting a great survey is not difficult at all. Often it is teamwork that impresses customers. Any dealership can have one good employee. If the customer meets or witnesses numerous employees who all seem to be equally as good, it will carry more weight. There is something about a group of people who work together appearing happy, positive, and supportive that elevates a satisfactory experience to the level of excellent.

Many times I would go into the box or shake the hand of the customer as he was leaving, offering a few words: "Mr. Customer, thanks again for your business. I just wanted to thank you personally. Your salesperson worked really hard for you. He's been doing an excellent job of changing the way we do business here. How was it for you?"

After being thanked when it is not expected, the customer will most likely speak well of the experience. They are happy. After all, they are buying or have just bought the car. They must like the salesperson a wee bit.

Once they have spoken nicely of the salesperson I add, "That's great to hear. If you truly enjoyed working with your salesperson please do him a favor without his knowledge. I'd like to keep him working here. It seems only people who are unhappy with their shopping experiences write letters to the owner. Your salesperson just had a run of bad luck. It would do him well if you could write a letter mentioning your experience today." I write the owner's name on the back of my business card and hand it to the customer. "If you need anything at all do not hesitate to call me. My direct extension is on the front. Thanks again."

Here's what happened. The customer made a statement that his experience was good to validate his reason for buying. Once they've done that they will need to back their statement up with a letter as to not seem hypocritical. After the letter is written and mailed they will get a survey in the mail. If they do not complete and send in the survey then their statement and their letter are of questionable validity.

The customer has agreed to take care of the salesperson who returns to complete the delivery. Make sure you are efficient and smile with good eye contact. The customer, right now, is deciding if he is writing the letter. He will decide quickly.

Get the customer smiling and wait for him to leave. Stand behind his car while he drives away, waving until you can no longer see him.

Congratulations! You Sold a Car

I watched the 1977 World Series as a young boy. It was October 18. Rookie manager Tommy Lasorda lead the Los Angeles Dodgers against the New York Yankees in the sixth game of the series. I'll never forget that game, and watching as Reggie Jackson came up to bat for the first time that night. There was something in the way he stood. Sure enough, he swung at the first pitch and it was gone.

During the fifth inning Reggie came up again. He seemed even more confident. His stance seemed looser. His eyes were fixed beyond the fence. Once again, the first pitch came and he swung. The ball was gone. He rounded the bases with a comfortable trot.

His third time up, the bases were loaded. It was the eighth inning. He swaggered up to the plate as confident as any man could be. His motion looked as if it were already footage from the evening news highlights. The moment was perfect. He couldn't miss. The first pitch came in slow motion. Camera flashes filled the stands. Neither the swing nor the ball could be seen. A grand slam.

Three home runs in one game. Amazing. I remember eating Reggie candy bars for the rest of my childhood. Since that day nothing has ever tasted as sweet.

Now get to work. It's time. The best time to sell a car is when you've just finished selling one. You're on top of your game. Nothing can bring you down. The customer can say "no" a thousand times and you will not listen. You don't have to listen. Today you have already succeeded in doing what you planned on doing. You sold a car.

They won't name a candy bar after you. Who cares? They'll talk about you for years if you sell every car on the lot.

Part V
Knowing Your Prospects

o o o o o o o o o o o o o o o o o o o o o o o o o o o o o o o o o

"If you can't gross your friends and family who can you gross?"

—Unknown

Sell Them All

How do we get our customers and where do they come from?

A good dealer invests in his community. I use the word invests because he expects a return for what he puts out. Maybe he supports his child's ballet class or baseball team. Do you think that the only reason he does that is to ensure that his loins are given the best position? I'm sure that is not the only reason. Couple this with the ego rush of seeing his name or the name of his business on ball caps and programs and you still have not completely listed his motivations. Add to this an opportunity to bring every one of the people involved in these activities into his dealership and now you have a portion of what moves him. These people within his circle have families, friends, and neighbors.

You have similar people involved in your family's daily lives. The social circles you are a part of could be fruitful if handled well. Let these people know what you do for a living. Talk in their luncheons. Offer your help when they want to buy a vehicle, even if it isn't your brand. Your willingness to help them unselfishly will lead you to find that many of them will choose to buy from you instead.

Common ground has been established. All we must know how to do is exploit it.

I was once told to sheer these people like a herd of sheep. You can skin them and they will warm you with their production once. If you sheer them a little here and a little there, you can return to them whenever necessary and use them for as long as they are alive.

What of the people that we don't have a relationship with? What kind of money and energy does it take to bring them into your place of business? They don't just happen to walk by and think to themselves, "Gee, I'll buy a car." They have been force fed product information in their daily lives. Their wants have been inflated with every magazine they read, channel they turn to, freeway they drive down, and radio station they listen to.

The buildup may have taken years. They systematically stop changing the oil in their car. Their tires are bald. Windshield is cracked. They don't need to maintain their car. They'll replace it instead, someday soon.

Americans are programmed to waste. Visit a garage sale this weekend and watch as families sell hundreds of dollars worth of stuff they bought for pennies on the dollar. Most of the junk that is for sale has been purchased within the same year it is being sold. I wouldn't doubt if much of the garage sale merchandise is still being paid for on somebody's revolving credit card account with a hefty interest rate.

These people who come in are not free. They cost about $300 apiece. Every time someone walks in to buy a soda or pick up a brochure, know that money was spent to get them there. This is money that the dealer wants back. It is money that you deserve. Don't waste your opportunities. Sell the guy that wants to walk through your showroom to use the restroom. Don't you think he's ready for a new car?

A recent report stated that the all-time best selling music album had just been outsold. The new leader reached 2 percent of the world's population! Think of your average American. Half the country is dumber than that man. The way I see it, there is another 48 percent out there that may buy a car instead of taking a crap in your two-star restroom.

Okay, You Let Them Get Away

The reality is you cannot sell them all when you first meet them. People have to leave. They find excuses to run and we buy in. We know that the majority of them will not come back. Out of this fear we let too many leave. Are we afraid that we may push that small percentage to an extreme and we lose them altogether, keeping them from returning? Why focus our energy on such a small number?

You won't. You're going to spend your time stopping the customer from leaving first and foremost. We're going after the 90 percent of customers who don't return. But there will be downtime. Time that you should use prospecting instead of hiding in a break room filling your face with quarter pounders.

It's time to schedule appointments to bring them back. Appointments have significantly higher closing ratios than first-time prospects. Typical appointments close 50 percent of the time. Bring them back and you have a great opportunity. Fill your weekday mornings with appointments and you will easily lead the rest of the dealership, if not the world, in sales volume.

The first time I call a prospect is directly after he leaves the dealership. Usually while they are driving home I place the first call. This is the only message I choose to leave on an answering machine: "Hi. This is Tony Z from Easy Eddie's. I have great news. Call me as soon as you get this message. (800) 555-1212. Thanks."

This message gets a phone call almost every time. The time the call comes can give insight as to what the customer was doing after he left the dealership. They may have given an excuse to leave that contradicts what they actually did (or say they did) after they left.

Maybe they returned home quicker than their excuse had set up for them. This could suggest that they found the vehicle or salesperson that they want to buy. Maybe that eludes to the fact that they have chosen you and your dealership. Good information, if you know it and can use it when the negotiation begins.

When they call back I say the same thing every time: "I am going through a list of people I met today who I really enjoyed working with. You are at the top of my list. I'd like to set an appointment where we can discuss your new car. When would you like to do this?" Then I shut up and listen.

The customers will direct me as to what they want to do. No matter what they say I remind myself that I must set an appointment. I listen to them and then set an appointment to discuss their situation.

There are people who will tell you that they do not wish to buy your car. They prefer another make or model. Set the appointment to bring them in and discuss this as well as talk about the other vehicle. Tell them that it is okay if they don't buy your car, but you do not want them to be taken advantage of. If they have a trade, tell them that you want to look at it again for more money. Use fear to further your chances. You're here to help them no matter what they decide to purchase. Often these people will come see you before they do anything. You're back in the game.

I've had customers call me from the F&I offices of other dealerships wanting to know if the figures were right or the deal they were about to sign for was good. What a wonderful position to be in. Another opportunity to schedule an immediate appointment with people that are ready to pull the trigger.

Sometimes the customer comes back to you because the other salesperson whom they had planned on purchasing from did not call them back. They want to feel good about their decision to buy and the other guy did not make them feel like they were worth a phone call. They bought a car that was their second or third choice simply because they weren't treated like they thought they should be. Whenever I see a vehicle that is poorly manufactured stuck on the side of the road I think about the salesperson and the job he must have done to put these folks together.

Phone Skills

Remember the presentation stage of the steps to the sale? That is where I mentioned value and how you must get your customers to use their senses in order to help build that value. This is one reason why we cannot sell anything over the phone. We have no control. We move ourselves to the next stage and begin doing what we do: defining the vehicle. We are trying to land the customer on the car they are inquiring about. We cannot land a person based solely on verbal influences. It is within the non-verbal signals that the verbal statements are more clearly understood.

Naturally, what are the next steps? Are we going to come to a point where the vehicle is so well defined that the customer says to us, "Okay, yes that is the one. How much?" You bet we are. How do we get out of that hole once we're there? It's difficult to do without losing credibility. I'm sure many sales professionals may be able to do so, but why would you want to have to do something that you had the choice not to do at all? Why spend time digging yourself out of a grave you shouldn't have dug for yourself to begin with? This is one area where the expression "work smart and not hard" is appropriate.

We can hit them over the phone with the manufacturer's suggested retail price as a number. What are our odds of them coming in of we do? What kind of energy does it take for them to call another dealer? We can low ball them and deal with the heat when they show up, screaming like a castrated teenager on the showroom floor. At least you brought them in, right? Or we can stay out of this situation by knowing it is possible for us to arrive here by asking the wrong questions or allowing ourselves to lose control of the deal.

What if we do not have the car? Here we go getting all the facts out. When the customer shows up, we are without what we already allowed the customer to tell us he wanted. We were not able to nix an item or items that our vehicle in stock does not have. We had to allow them to speak. Their speaking and our passivity supported their decision early on. Now it is a must item for them. We've buried their seed in concrete. It's going to take a bit of work to dig this one up. Again, why work hard and not smart?

Do not continue in this manner. You do not want to go through each step to the sale over the phone. You will not be able to have the customer take delivery of the vehicle over the phone. They cannot pay for it, sign the proper paperwork, or drive it home. You want the customer right there in front of you. Period.

In California, where I work in the business, there are laws which allow for any customer who completes paperwork and takes delivery away from the dealership three days to bring that vehicle back. By the time I'm done with my customers there is so much ether around them that I have at least a day before they call me with a question or two. I think the only way that I won't hear from them within three days is if they feel that I might have made a mistake and sold the car too cheap. They don't want to bring it back. Otherwise, if I sold them a vehicle for sticker or more they may stop at another store, or at the very least, wake up. I don't want to worry about this in any way. I want to be done with them.

Once again, telling isn't selling.

As salespeople we are programmed to respond in a specific way when a customer shows interest in a vehicle. If that interest is verbal and over the phone, we naturally make very little distinction. We go for the close. What good does that do us without someone we can touch in front of us?

So what do you do? Start by not answering the phone. Remember, "If you cannot say anything nice do not say anything at all." I would say lying over the phone is definitely not being nice to the customer, and giving away the dealer's profit is not nice to the dealer.

There are various scripts that you can read and training sessions that you can attend. I have attended a few of them myself. I can say that I have found merit in all of the ones I have encountered. They give us a plan which we can stick to. Any training and execution of a plan is better than no training and no execution whatsoever. If we have a map and know how to read it, we will find our way into the city.

I use a very simple routine every time I answer the phone. My routine is based on customers who are calling for information on vehicles. They are possible sales calls only. A typical call goes something like this:

"Thank you for calling Easy Eddie's. You're calling because of the big sale, right?"

"Yes."

"I'm sorry. I didn't hear that. Could you hold please?"

(Customer is on hold for five seconds, no longer, no matter what they say)

"Thanks for holding. Are you calling because of the big sale?"

"Yes. Do you have a Yada Yada?"

"Do you prefer new or used?"

(It doesn't matter what they say.)

"I'm sorry. I'm being pulled in four different directions right now. The big sale has caught us off guard. I believe we have what you are looking for. We usually do. Do you know where we are at?"

"Yes."

"Good." (I give them directions anyway.) "Are you calling from home or work?"

(They look around at their surroundings and answer.)

"Where is that?"

(They tell you.)

"Take this road to that road and then turn left and pull into our parking lot. Walk in like you own the place and ask for Tony Z. If you cannot find a spot to park here, call me on my cell phone and I'll come pick you up, wherever you park. Do you have a pen? I'll wait."

(They get a pen.)

"My number is (800) 555-1212. My name is Tony Z. Always ask for me. Please. I'm trying to help a customer. I'm sorry, someone is pulling at the phone. Are you coming now or is this something that can wait until the sale is over?"

"I'm on my way" or "I'll be there tonight" or "When does it end?" or "I can wait."

No matter what they say, your mission is to set an appointment and bring them in. Make it sound like the dealership has been overrun by customers and the sale is ending today. If they can wait, then their interest is not something I am very motivated by or interested in. However, I put the uninterested people on hold again for another five seconds.

"I'm going to put some time aside for you so you may have my undivided attention and I'll be ready to help you when you arrive. You spell your name...?"

(They'll spell it out for you.)

"You'll be arriving at what time?"

(They'll tell you.) "4:00 o'clock."

"Oh. That doesn't work. I'll be delivering another car. Can we make it 4:30?"

"Sure."

"Great Mr. Customer, I look forward to seeing you at 4:30 this afternoon. Still have that pen?"

"Yes."

"My number is (800) 555-1212. If something should change could you give me the courtesy of a phone call?"

"Yes."

"Great. And if something should change on my part, I'll do the same. Your number is?"

This is where it becomes interesting. Customers will give you their number if they are coming in. They will not if they are not hooked. For those who give their number I repeat the time we will meet and my name, and thank them for calling. Anybody who does not continue, I apologize and ask them to "Please hold once more" and I turn the phone over to someone else whom I have worked this same routine with. That salesman will try the same routine.

Everything that is stated is said as if the dealership is swarming with people and I must get off as soon as possible to help these customers. True. The customer on the phone is as important as our fictitious customers on the showroom floor, but they do have one thing in common: neither of them can buy a car where they are at.

Your Role & Responsibilities

I call on dealerships regularly. It is appalling how poorly handled the phones are. Either the phone system itself is an impersonal recorder that spins me off into "permanent ignore" or the employees are not properly trained. It is typically one or the other. Many times it's both.

I understand that it is not easy to find good quality phone help for the wages dealers wish to pay people who are not on commission. Isn't it strange that dealers will spend tens of thousands of dollars every month on advertising, which only creates 10 percent of their total business, yet they want to pay some college student or retiree minimum wage for part-time work as the first person a prospect hears when he calls in?

You have a responsibility whenever you answer the phone. The person calling in must hear a pleasant sounding voice. A voice that makes the customer say to themselves, "Sounds like a happy person. Must be a wonderful place to work." I'm not talking about a person who monotonously states the same greeting every time. Or someone who reads a script that fulfills the dealer's ego rather than creates a pleasant sounding atmosphere.

What can you do? Remember that if you pick up the phone you are responsible to ensure that the caller reaches whomever he wants to speak with. Do not just transfer the call back into some terminal sitting on some desk hoping it will get answered. Put the customer on hold. Call back prior and make sure someone will pick the call up. If there is no response then take a message by hand and walk it to the co-worker, or at the very least, your desk manager. More importantly, get the call handled.

If you do your share, maybe the dealer will do his. There are some dealers who have eight car lines and attempt to put them all in the greeting. If you are one of these dealers you should know that if it takes three breaths from the receptionist to finish the greeting, then it may be a bit too long. Consider shortening it.

Recorded greetings that answer the phones automatically are overrated. There is nothing like the personal touch and sound of a happy voice. If you are a dealer and are tired of hearing about phone concerns, try this: Unplug your automated system for three months. Pay your top salesperson his average monthly earnings for the time period. Have them work the phone with the understanding that if there are fewer problems and sales increase, you will increase their pay by 10 percent of the total gross increase that you realized. See if this makes a difference.

Games People Play

o o o o o o o o o o o o o o o o o o o o o o o o o o o o o o o o o o

"Keep your friends close. Keep your enemies closer."

—*Sun Tzu*
The Art of War

The remaining portions of this book are here to share some basic common sense beliefs that I have about concerns not typically mentioned. Some of the concerns are put in story format and do not have a place within the previous chapters. Each is important for its own specific lesson.

These stories are here for your enjoyment as well. You may not find your typically humorous or enjoyable story, yet they contain elements that helped me become the salesperson I am today. Most of these topics were taken directly out of my personal journal, written during my first year in the business. I have changed the names only. The rest is true. These are some of the games that people play.

Getting Rid of Competition

I hated them. Yes, hated. As strong as a word as hate is, it is exactly what I felt for Mark and Cody.

I didn't hate them for anything they did to me. Nor were they in any way villains in the normal sense of the word. They were my only competition. Their sales numbers kept me from getting the bonus money or the nice car to drive. Their existence in the dealership threatened my position because I felt more expendable than I would have preferred to feel.

Cody strutted around the dealership, always laughing for unknown reasons, like he owned the place. His nose was high and he would not give any assistance whenever I asked for help. He did not like working for half deals and would not accept a turn from me unless I relinquished the entire deal to him.

One of Cody's hobbies became his failure within the store. He was proud of his golf game. So much so that every discussion had to stop somewhere around how the greens were the day before or how he improved his swing. As part of his normal working attire he carried a golf ball which he bounced incessantly, while he walked around the showroom and chatted with co-workers.

Mark was an annoying guy with few friends. We shared an office together. He stood at an average height and looked every bit like the All-American boy next door. His love was his ten-year-old car, a German import with a stereo that cost more than the car when it was new and before it had a billion miles on it. Each night at closing he would drive that vehicle, bouncing and thumping up to the customer parking area, while I helped with the chore of locking up.

At this particular dealership we each had been assigned a dealer plate to use for demonstration drives. The management enjoyed a weekly ritual of asking every salesperson to bring his or her plate into their office to be inventoried. Those salespeople that did not produce a plate would be fined $100.

Most of the salespeople were good about keeping track of where their plate was. I always had mine. Mark had his. Cody was the exception. He was flighty and would leave his plate laying around wherever he was at when he began to work his deals. I know he figured it would be there when he returned. It usually was.

One day I found Cody sitting in my office. He was on the telephone, bouncing that damn golf ball on my desk beside his dealer plate. He did not turn to see me waiting to use my office. When his phone call ended he stood, still preoccupied with the conversation he had finished, and took his golf ball. His plate remained on my desk.

By the luck of things, he did not need his plate for the rest of the day. I went ahead and stuck it between the wall and my personal belongings, figuring he'd be looking for it soon enough. He never looked and I didn't bother to tell him.

The next day Mark took a turn from me. I could not get the customer to commit and spun the deal while in the box. Mark made the deal, and much to my surprise decided to forget how he'd come upon the customer. He demanded the entire deal and was rewarded it without any further consideration from the desk manager.

Mark's demands within the sales office, as well as a bit of fate, sparked what would happen next. Being somewhat put off by the thievery, I took a drive. There was a country club parking lot I enjoyed stopping at from time to time for breaks. The scenery was always conducive to meditating and reviewing the day's events. When I parked in my usual space I happened to notice a golf ball sitting beside a parking curb. It took only moments for me to retrieve the ball and return to the back lot where we employees parked our cars.

Mark's car was parked where I usually park. His driver side window was shattered. I did not know how this happened, but was sure that it had been done intentionally. He had his share of enemies. I dropped the golf ball on the seat in a pile of broken glass and walked at a normal pace back to the comfort of the line to get an up. I do not recall how long it took for Mark to find his window shattered, but I remember that it happened after a group of us watched Cody walk up from the employee lot, talking on his cell phone through a giggling fit. Another salesperson came up directly after Cody and mentioned the window to Mark, who ran back there at that moment.

When Mark returned with a golf ball in his hands the store was in an uproar. He tore into the showroom and went from office to office, searching for Cody.

One of the managers headed out to stop him. The other manager, who might have been trying to get some control of the rest of the salespeople by distracting them, paged over the intercom, "All sales personnel...please bring your dealer plates to the office." I went into my office and dropped Cody's dealer plate in Mark's briefcase while collecting mine for review.

Cody looked very nervous, hastily bouncing around looking for his plate. He was still unaware that Mark was searching for him throughout the dealership.

It was a mess when they found each other. The circumstantial evidence was enough to cause chaos. I'm still unclear on whether they were fired or quit. I never learned who actually broke Mark's window. I do know that I have not seen either of the two since that day, and I was able to climb back onto half of my deal.

__Friends__

It must be brought up. There is a place and a time for everything and everyone. The place to discuss friendship is here and not in the dealership.

The comradery that close quarters and shared experience creates is strong. The desire for others to accept us is natural. It is not an easy process to walk through this world, where people are free with their opinions on what a car salesperson is or should be. We feel the need to surround ourselves with others like us, who accept us for who we are.

Many of my closest friends I have met while working in the business. We've played poker, seen movies, gone fishing, broke bread, enjoyed each other's company away from the dealership on regular occasions. Our wives and families have spent time together. Every one of them has at one point or another weaseled his way into my commission or stolen a deal from me and my family.

Why is it that we can so easily be social with people that have the tendency toward this type of behavior? Does money truly change people, or do people not change until money is involved? I believe it is the latter of the two.

This does not mean that I do not maintain friendships with those who have stolen from me. On the contrary, I have learned what they are capable of. If I were to end a relationship with them once I realized their potential, I would not have the opportunity to get my money back. Often, while waiting for a chance to vindicate my pocketbook I find that our wives have scheduled a night out.

Relationships are not perfect. Even the longest lasting marriages have their ups and downs. It is weighing the bad with the good and knowing what can be achieved if we continue to remain together as friends. Someone will always have to give in to the other's will. A compromise between two people is a greater concession on the part of one person. The other person involved must be allowed to impose his will, this time.

As you or your friend is promoted, the dynamics of your relationship will change. It will have to in order to ensure your mutual success. One of you is going to supervise the other at some point. What information about you and your private life would you like your supervisor to know? How about your wife or your children? Is their relationship with your friends family going to haunt you? How will your life need to change in the future if you allow yourself to be seen too closely early on in the relationships that you build today?

Time Issues

While a member of my high school wrestling team, I heard a story about a remarkable man. His name is Dan Gable and his story helped lay a foundation for who I am today.

It is said that Mr. Gable made excellent use of his time. Not only did he train after his team had quit for the day, but he continued to train to a fanatical extent. While attending movies and theater with his peers he would become antsy. The concern on his face would show and he would begin to run up and down the aisles, seemingly overcome by energy. His peers thought this odd and would often ask him why he was doing this. He responded, "My opponent is not resting."

Time management changed for me around the time that I first heard this story. I have put my time into understandable measures, graded within the same scale which I was accustomed to during school. This grading has carried through to my sales career and is probably the single most driving element of my psyche.

I ask myself throughout my day what grade of time I am spending with each task. If I am with a customer, in any position close enough that they can hand me a check, then I am spending "A" quality time with them. This is the time that I prefer to fill my day with. Without it I am not capable of working on commission.

"B" time could be any time that can produce "A" time at a moment's notice. Walking the service department, trolling the lot, and parading around the parking area are all good examples of "B" time. This is due to the possibility of shaking a customer's hand and beginning to plant seeds for a deal.

If I find myself doing chores such as visiting the parts department to get a price on a part for a customer or sending letters to prospects or customers, then I call that time "C" time. It is essential time that is used to keep others happy. It does not immediately pay my bills this month, but it may come around to help me in the future. Remember, my time is about me.

Taking breaks and chatting with coworkers is either "F" time or "D" time depending on where I am doing these things and how I am using this time. Perhaps I am off sight having lunch by myself. Maybe I'm reading a book, unrelated to sales. If I don't talk to anybody about what they drive, then I feel I am wasting time.

There is a balance, though. We must take a break to relax our minds. The few minutes away from the grind is beneficial to everyone. Your manager and coworkers need to have you out of their faces for a few minutes every day. The change in actors on a stage is always pleasing to the audience as well as other actors involved. New stories are formed which can be shared later.

I encourage you to watch your time consciously. Eat before and after your scheduled shift. If you must stop during the day, try to pick a time when the floor is covered with salespeople and customers are nowhere to be found. Eat when the desk manager eats and your deal will have the proper attention when he is not eating.

Try using your break time outdoors. Walk the dealership with the idea that it is your break. If you happen to run into a customer while on break, you can let them know in a manner that is beneficial to you. Tell them that you would love to help them. You're not as important as they are. Besides, with the two of you just chatting about vehicles and looking around it is just as easy to relax. Maybe they'll drop their guard and give you some useful information. Some of the biggest sales vouchers I've had started while I was on a break.

A harder time to schedule is family time. I try to make sure that I have arranged all I can for my scheduled work time, but the customers buy cars when they want to, not always when I want to sell them. Do not tell a customer that you are off tomorrow so they'll have to wait a few days for you. They may find this appropriate at the time you say it and agree to do so. I guarantee that the next day or hour they will be at my dealership attempting to justify their buying decision with you. If they are, you're dead. Sell them now.

Tell the customer that you do not want them to waste any more of their valuable time having to leave and return, only to purchase the same car for a different price tomorrow or the next day. Make it about them. I tell a story about a time when a customer missed an opportunity.

My manager walked with me to his car when he was taking the weekend off. On our walk he was discussing the importance of the dealership selling three more specific model units by Sunday evening. These vehicles had to be reported to the manufacturer by 9 p.m. in order for the dealership to collect a retroactive dealer payment equal to about $50,000, of which I would get my little piece.

During the sales meeting that I held about ten minutes after he had left, I put a healthy spiff on the sale of these models. The salespeople were motivated and went to the phones. That Friday evening we sold one of these cars, leaving two to go.

Saturday was uneventful for that model. Although many salespeople tried, nobody could spark an interest in these units. Seeing that the salespeople were now in poorer spirits regarding their attempts, I placed another group of bonuses for the demonstration and write-up of the units on Sunday. It worked. We were driving people throughout the day but not getting them on paper.

At noon, a repeat customer came in asking for a salesperson whom he'd purchased from time and again. The customer did not know what he wanted to buy. He only knew that he wanted to replace both his and his wife's cars. It was a dream come true. We drove them in the models and they loved them.

Putting the customer on paper, my excitement for the sale was obvious to my salesperson. He already knew that I wanted them moved badly due to the hefty spiff I had placed on these units. Unfortunately, he telegraphed this in some manner to the customer, who began to lean back in his chair.

The dealership closed around the customer, and still no bending to give a workable commitment. My closer was beat red and I went in to see what the true holdup was. The customer told me that he knew there was "lots of money" riding on this deal.

"Okay," I said. "Tell me what you think we are in for."

My commitment came in the form of a five thousand dollar under invoice deal on each vehicle. I was thinking, "That's a total ten thousand dollar gift for him and forty thousand for the dealership." Something told me not to do it. Something wasn't right. I pondered it briefly and gave a final, realistic offer. The customer refused and stood to leave.

I said, "Sir. Please understand that this deal is good only today."

"Augh," he quipped back, "if you can do it today you can do it tomorrow," and walked out.

Upon my manager's return the following day I told him the story of this deal. The manager opened his incentive book and read through the rules to see if he had made a mistake. Maybe we could find a loophole. Sure enough a mistake had been made. We did not need three units when he left Friday, but four. Had I sold the cars I would have lost $10,000 for the dealership.

As a side note, guess who walked into our office not ten minutes later. That's right: Mr. Customer. "Okay! You're my man," he said while pointing at me. "Let's do those deals."

It gave me great pleasure to say, "Sorry. The program ended yesterday."

I won't continue with how we sold this man two different cars, but I will say that he wished he'd believed us when we said, "The numbers are good today only."

Owning Porters

Probably the hardest working individual in any dealership is the porter. He's the guy who washes your deliveries and maintains an organized, clean facility for you to work in. His happiness is important since he holds the keys to your customers' impressions of the dealership, both when they arrive as well as when they drive off in their new cars. If this man does not care for you, then you will often find your vehicles being ignored prior to delivery.

Subsequently, if this person likes you, then not only will your deliveries be prepared in a timely fashion, but their attention to detail will be evident. If the vehicle is missing something that it should have, like floor mats, or it has minor lot damage, you may see the porter taking care of you by going the extra mile.

It doesn't take much to get these guys to perform. They want to be given the respect they deserve and not treated like they're worthless. Sound familiar? We need to apply the golden rule here. Remember to ask them for help and not try to tell them what to do.

They are making the lowest wage in the dealership. Much like the phone personnel that we discussed earlier. Isn't it peculiar that the people who have the greatest control when it comes to manipulating the perceptions of customers toward positive satisfaction are paid the least as well as walked on the most?

I buy my porters lunch whenever I buy my team members lunch. If I am eating and they enter the break room I ask them to sit with me (or ask them if I may sit with them if the opposite occurs). When they are walking about and I am having a conversation with other team members I make sure that I include them. Occasionally, on their birthdays, their anniversaries, and Christmas, I give them a "C" note.

My porters remember me.

Sales Satisfaction Surveys

In many other business models it is becoming increasingly popular to ask customers for their input via surveys. This is not something that is new to those of us in the automotive business. The manufacturers have been using this type of device as an excuse as well as a vehicle for controlling dealerships for quite some time.

There are many dealerships who have poor survey scores on a regular basis. I believe that these folks should lose some privileges here and there in regards to factory monies. Unfortunately it is not always the case. It seems that those with the greatest sales volume and who have the money make the rules. No survey changes that.

The survey does come into play when the manufacturer has its feet held to the fire. Then they do something about it. Not like they didn't try. They usually try but are not capable of solving issues when the dealer body holds the cards to their success.

It is within the dealerships that want to listen to the customer that the surveys work. If the dealership itself reads every written comment, whether positive or negative, they can begin to trend issues relative to customer satisfaction. Through time these trends will offer input as to many factors on the sales floor. Surveys from outsiders can give information relevant to both the way customers are handled as well as overall internal morale.

Unfortunately the current model for the Sales Satisfaction Survey is poor. It usually has only five available responses. The calculation is just that, math. There is no area for handwritten human involvement. Strange how it takes significantly more time for a person to think about what they want to write and then write it than it takes for them to fill in a little bubble and go on with their lives, yet the value of the customer who does so is lost.

Add to this the ease of mailing the device, and who is predisposed to actually doing so, and the numbers become further from the truth. Those that are mad are infested with the same motivators as anyone who has committed a crime of passion. Their motivation is the defense mechanism that cannot believe that they were taken. They were mistreated by standards that were put in to place by their own expectations, however distorted they might be. Someone has made them look or feel foolish. We send these customers surveys and ask them to return them, oftentimes paying the postage ourselves.

What of the happy customers? Is it as easy for them to give 100 percent as it is for the pissed off customer to give us a zero? Not likely. Nobody's perfect, right?

Yet in the eyes of manufacturers as well as outside private survey companies who advertise the results of the surveys, there is no acceptable answer less than perfect.

Are we so good as a business that we deserve marks of 100 percent? I think not. What can we learn by getting these marks? There is something and some way we can improve if the marks allow for 80 percent as a passing grade. Then the perfect score would give insight as to how the customer really felt.

If manipulation alone is what the manufacturers want of the numbers, as it appears to be, then there are ways of cheating. However, we are cheating ourselves. Keep in mind that we will not learn how to improve by finishing our duties this way. We will only make others feel good about whatever job they are doing.

Getting perfect scores on the survey is simply a matter of programing. As mentioned earlier in the "Delivery" portion of the book, you can program the customer to respond favorably.

Blind Truck Buyer

I try to cover each customer the same way in many portions of the deal. There are words I do not use and statements that I do not make. They have been removed from my repertoire intentionally so I know that I will not hang myself with them at some point. By completing specific jobs with specific words we offer ourselves many advantages. The following story illustrates that you never know what you may find out until you ask hundreds of customers the same question.

It was a weekday when I met Joe Customer. He walked in and began asking questions about trucks. You couldn't tell that he was blind by the way he looked. It wasn't until the demonstration drive that he told me.

I tried to switch places with him at a nice point along my route. He turned me down in a matter-of-fact way. He had mentioned that his wife would be the primary driver earlier on, but that never stops me from trying to sell someone whom I have in front of me.

No problem. I drove and he rode. We discussed his wife, who was "out of town." She would be back the following weekend. She was to return late Friday night. He felt that she wouldn't be ready to shop until Saturday morning. I scheduled our appointment and gave the man no numbers to shop.

I said, as I always do, "Remember: Always check with me last. All my customers do. I don't care what you buy or from whom you buy it. I just want you to be treated fairly. If you don't check with me last, you'll always wonder if you paid too much."

I was off Friday night. My wife and I went to see a movie. I remember coming home to a page that showed the dealership's phone number. It was late and the store was closed so I didn't return the call. Besides, I'd be there by noon the next day.

Saturday morning I headed in to work a couple hours early. Upon arrival I was approached by a co-worker who informed me that my customers were in the night before, Joe and his wife. They were going to be back with me today at our previously scheduled time to talk some numbers.

I'm a nice guy. I believe in the old saying of "what goes around comes around." I like when customers that I have worked with ask for me and I like it when other salespeople help me out instead of cutting me up. Since my co-worker helped them, he was on half the deal. I told him so and he thanked me.

Joe Customer and his wife came in as scheduled. I always start my deals from square one when I have be-backs, to ensure that the ether builds back up. I make sure that I haven't missed anything while I build value in the vehicle. We took a test drive and completed the deal in a very hasty manner. There wasn't much discussion and the customers were in the finance department.

In between the paperwork and getting the vehicle ready my co-worker popped his head in and thanked me for "finishing them off."

Once the customer was ready we sat to review the sales satisfaction survey. My canned portion of the review stated, "If for any reason you did not like me, or my co-worker who you worked with last night…"

I was stopped with a bewildered look from Joe Customer's wife. "Who?"

"You were here last night. Weren't you?" I asked.

"No. I called last night to let you know my wife was in and confirm our appointment with you today," the husband said.

"Okay," I continued, "if for any reason you did not like me, you may go ahead and toss that survey in the trash. No. I'm kidding. Don't do it. It'll kill me…" I went on like I'd misstated. I do not want the customer to feel awkward in any manner. I'll handle any concern of mine later, after the customer leaves.

They left happy in their new truck. I returned to the sales manager's desk, where he was recapping the deal and handing out vouchers to both of the salespeople involved in the deal.

While my co-worker stood next to me I asked him, "So, did they enjoy the way it drove last night?"

"Yes," he hesitated.

"He loved it when I drove him," I said.

"Yes. He really enjoyed the way it felt when he drove it with me, too," my co-worker responded.

"Funny," I said while walking out of the sales office, "he's blind. He doesn't drive."

My point was not to get my half of the deal back, though I did manage to do so by making this statement in front of the sales manager. Instead, I wished to inform my coworker of the fact that I knew he was lying. The fear he would carry would weigh strongly whenever I was not around. He would not press his luck in the future. He now knew that pigs get fat, but hogs get slaughtered.

Continued Sales Training

You've made it! You've reached the end of the book. Like I stated earlier, one of my goals in writing this book was to make sure that you were able to complete it. I do not wish to help you begin your new career with a failure caused by you not being able to finish these fundamentals. Pat yourself on the back, as you now have a useful foundation on which to begin your new role.

Though armed with the tools, you will need to continue your daily practice of them. Professional athletes do not stop practicing. Neither should you.

Use the green peas to practice with whenever possible. This affords you many opportunities. First and foremost, you will hear new objections which they find difficult to overcome. These roadblocks give you the chance to prepare as well as look very good to an easily influenced peer. Being around these green peas, you will feed off their positive attitude as well as their turns. If enough of them come through your dealership, eventually a few of them will stick around a while. This group of people becomes your people when you are promoted.

That's why you're doing this today. You want to make as much money as you can while learning a business that will advance you in time. You want someone to recognize how well you perform and reward you for it. With enough smart work you can get the rewards you will deserve.

If your only wish is to be a great salesperson, that is respectable. Be the best in your store. In order to remain on top you will need to continue your training. You must not stop at what you know. Customers change with the weather and what you may learn from fresh approaches and new ideas can potentially be the difference between enjoying what you do and doing nothing.

Buy books and encourage your peers, co-workers, managers, and dealer principals to do the same. If everyone in your workplace were to read the same training materials which you have read, different ideas will be found. Talk about the books you read amongst your team and grow together. These small circles of ideas promote positive team cohesion. Together you will be invincible.

Attend sales training seminars regularly. Being around others who wish to better themselves is a learning experience in and of itself. The comradery that exists in these training groups is worth its weight in gold. You never know who you may be associating with and when you will need that person to help you out of a bind.

There are far too many training seminars to choose from. While running a dealership I had little time to spend answering phone calls from every sales trainer that had a "new approach." They all called on me in the same manner. I was unclear as to how their new approach fit into their daily routine, as it did not fit into mine. If I had answered many of their calls I would have had even less time to spend focusing on the actual sales training of my sales team.

For this reason I do not hunt out training opportunities like the conventional trainers do. Instead I believe that the cream rises to the top. I am the cream. There are ways for you to reach me no matter who you are. I answer every inquiry myself.

If you would like to contact me directly I am available for individual tutoring or manufacturer training seminars as well as complete dealership training programs. Visit carsandpeople.net or send email to clozzzed@aol.com. At either place, you may leave comments, concerns, and kudos, and discuss consultation.

Thanks & Stay Tuned

The car business is a wonderful business to be in. It is not the feeling of the hunt as much as it is the kill which drives us. The immediate gratification that comes from work that we had no idea we would be doing when we arrived in the morning. We do not know which customers will visit or which of their concerns we will have the opportunity to overcome until we are faced with them. The pleasure of watching a customer drive off in a vehicle that he had no intention of buying swells our egos as well as our pocketbooks. It is fresh and rewarding every day that we approach it with a positive attitude. Success makes us smile.

Good luck and keep smiling!

Glossary

Be-back: A customer that has left and returns, or is expected to return. Someone who was doing all the selling while we were busy buying into his excuses.

Bump: We move our customers in bumps we take one at a time. Bumps in payment or down payment come one step at a time. If we ask for everything all at once our customer may become defensive and draw a line between you. It is often easier to push a man over a cliff if you get him to step back one step at a time while getting him comfortable within your conversation.

Buyer's Remorse: Known as the "BRs." After the ether fades, customers may wake up and begin to wonder how they will pay for what they just bought. Some people believe it is not a money issue alone. If this is so, then how would the customer feel if the item were free? Probably wouldn't have any remorse whatsoever. The remorse comes from having to be accountable for their decisions. Within the decision process we prefer to leave ourselves an out or create a scapegoat that allows us the opportunity to forgo any responsibility, preferring to blame others for our decision. While closing a deal it is a good idea to tell the customer this statement: "Okay. You want me to get this done, right?" I use this often within the close itself, allowing me the opportunity to help a customer with buyer's remorse if he tries to blame me later. I can easily answer, "I asked you if you wanted me to do that. You said yes, you did. I only did what you asked me to do."

Closer: The better qualified salesperson who finishes off the deal. The money man. Usually leads and trains a team of salespeople whose deals pay him a portion of whatever they produce.

Commitment: When a customer drives over the curb and you have his money.

Get-me-done: A customer who will pay what it takes at terms that are not typically in the customer's best interest just to drive out in a car.

Glue: Cash down payment. All monies used as the down payment that hold the deal together.

Green Pea: A new salesperson. The lowest position in a sales department, with the least respect. The person who does not know what he is incapable of. The person who goes blindly into every interaction, believing there is a chance for personal victory. The best thing that ever happened to a dealership. An impressionable, lucky, and positive influence on the sales floor.

Grinder: A customer who takes far too long to close. They are sometimes referred to this way because it seems that they pay too little profit. We forget that profit is not in their control. It's our responsibility to ensure an acceptable profit. We would rather call them a grinder than admit our weakness by saying "no" and stopping the deal sooner out of fear that we may lose it altogether.

Heat: Customer complaints. Not always an irate customer, but one that has the potential to be. Not something you would want to deal with during a time when you are busy. An often wasted opportunity to overcome objections after the sale has occurred. A chance to "look very good" and build a customer for life. Another way that a customer is brought to us by which we can improve the deal.

Laydown: A derogatory reference to a customer who does what we ask him to. Someone who goes our way the entire deal. Isn't it strange that we have such a poor word for a person whom we should adore?

Line: "The line" is given its name thanks to how closely it resembles a lineup. It's where we stand while waiting for the next customer. Too often we choose to stand next to each other, shooting the breeze while waiting for the customer to approach. This is very intimidating to the customer. Whenever I find myself standing in a group of other salespeople I try to remind myself that only one of us will be allowed to approach a customer. As numbers have it, I would prefer to be alone so I may be the only person who has the opportunity to begin my deal. Why allow competition when it is not necessary?

Lot Lizard: A customer who visits every lot for fun. Someone found always shopping at a dealership because he likes cars. An excuse for a salesperson as to why he didn't shut or turn the deal. An easy way to disregard an opportunity to sell a car.

Low-ball: A very low price. Sometimes this number is not a deal. It is intended to bring the customer back or screw up another dealer's deal. If you word it correctly when the customer is leaving, you can give the impression of a low-ball, stopping the customer and closing the deal immediately. It's acting at its finest whenever the customer buys into the "fact" that the price being counter-offered by you is lower than they will find anywhere else or any other day but today.

Marriage: Some stores have a marriage policy. Let's say that you are working with a customer and you cannot take that customer to the next step for some reason. You will need to turn that customer to another salesperson. While that salesperson is working your customer it is your responsibility to go get another up. You need to work a deal for that salesperson as well. You will each get half of each deal. You are married.

One-Legger: An excuse used by the salesperson for not taking a customer to the next step. One of the decision-makers is present while the other is not. *Example: "I didn't drive her because she is a one-legger. Her husband will come by tomorrow."*

Pencil: When the desk manager gives you numbers for your deal. The pencil is a written part of the deal. It comes with direction when a good desk manager is involved. He asks what was said and offers insight as to what you should do and say. Listen to this man when you get one who does this. Not all desk managers give the direction necessary with their pencil. These managers only help you half the way. These are the guys who believe deep down that it's all about the math. Your gross will eventually suffer.

Qualify: Something we do in an effort to short-cut our deals from the start. Our ability to know all allows us this unique talent of knowing when someone can and will buy a car without going through the steps of the sale.

Roach: A customer who has credit issues beyond what the desk manager believes he is capable of getting financed. An excuse for a desk manager or finance manager to kick someone out of the dealership without having to take a chance or work very hard. Someone who will pay whatever it takes but is often treated poorly due to laziness on the part of the sales staff.

Spiff: A bonus given by the dealership for a job well done. Something one should not take for granted. It is not an entitlement. A spiff is given for going over and above the call of duty. In war you get medals for this type of behavior. Here you get money.

Third Baseman: A customer's friend. Someone whom the customer puts great weight in. Someone the customer believes in. A crutch or security blanket for the customer. Someone who is not always used to our benefit. A person who can shut the deal with a simple nod of the head. Someone whom we could easily manipulate once we are aware of his individual motivations.

Tour: The foot route you take while bringing the customer into your office. A planned opportunity to continue building value while showing the conviction you have in your dealership.

Turn: (also referred to as "spinning") When a salesperson allows another salesperson an opportunity to make a deal. Usually a turn is done with the customer being introduced to the next salesperson. This allows for any transfer or buildup of credibility. An introduction would usually be something like, "This is Joe Customer. Joe, this is Bob Salesperson. He's been here longer and can address your concerns better. You're with the right guy now." Then the first salesperson would turn and walk away, relinquishing any control.

Unwind: A vehicle that comes back into inventory after driving off the lot with a customer. Usually unwinds are due to credit concerns. Typically there are very few miles on these units, but they can no longer be sold as "new" cars.

Up: A customer. Your opportunity at a deal. Someone to take seriously as you may not get another one for the rest of your shift.

0-595-32751-6

Printed in the United States
52981LVS00005B/55-60

9 780595 327515